Affirmative Action and the Meanings of Merit

Bruce P. Lapenson

UNIVERSITY PRESS OF AMERICA,® INC.
Lanham • Boulder • New York • Toronto • Plymouth, UK

Copyright © 2009 by
University Press of America,® Inc.
4501 Forbes Boulevard
Suite 200
Lanham, Maryland 20706
UPA Acquisitions Department (301) 459-3366

Estover Road
Plymouth PL6 7PY
United Kingdom

Library of Congress Control Number: 2008935974
ISBN-13: 978-0-7618-4347-4 (paperback : alk. paper)
ISBN-10: 0-7618-4347-7 (paperback : alk. paper)
eISBN-13: 978-0-7618-4348-1
eISBN-10: 0-7618-4348-5

∞™ The paper used in this publication meets the minimum
requirements of American National Standard for Information
Sciences—Permanence of Paper for Printed Library Materials,
ANSI Z39.48—1984

For my father and the memory of my mother

Contents

Introduction

This study defends affirmative action, and focuses on a crucial research question: Do traditional methods of selection in employment, higher education, and contracts assure African-Americans equal opportunity? The study will appraise the definition of merit and qualifications. Qualifications, as George Sher denotes, are the abilities necessary to perform a specific job: "No job can be done unless a worker has the requisite skill or ability, so the primary purpose of seeking someone to do a job will only be accomplished if one hires a suitably skilled applicant."[1] Michael Walzer suggests a similar premise: ". . . one really wants doctors and (even) civil servants to have certain sorts of qualifications."[2] Sher, however, argues that, among the skilled, there is a *most* skilled whom it is rational and fair to hire or admit.[3] Similarly, Terry Eastland claims that employers must hire, in order to be competitive, the ". . . outstanding . . ." [and] ". . . best . . ." applicants, rather than those who are qualified but "less qualified".[4]

Explicated in this way, qualifications are linked with the idea of merit or desert. Sher argues that the "best qualified" deserve or merit positions because such selection arrangements treat applicants as ". . . choosers and doers . . .," not ". . . as mere bearers of needs or claims, as passive links in casual claims, or as interchangeable specimens of larger groups or classes."[5] This perspective depicts the "best qualified" as the most deserving because to do otherwise disrespects the rational agency of individuals. Daniel Bell describes a meritocratic society as one where "men [are] judged and rewarded on the basis . . . of individual merit," and where "differential status and differential income are based on technical skills . . . and few high places are open to those without such qualifications."[6] Linking qualifications and desert connects the pragmatic with the moral; possessing the necessary skills for a specific position warrants *deserving* to be chosen before those who do not possess them, or before those who possess fewer of them. The proponents of meritocracy assume that the methods which determine qualifications—and extent of qualification—are objective. This study argues, conversely, that the academic, public, and political critiques of affirmative action do not prove the objectivity of traditional methods of recruitment and selection.

The linking of qualifications with desert is associated with classical liberal notions of equal opportunity. As Bell states, ". . . the individual . . . is the basic unit of society, and . . . the purpose of societal arrangements is to allow the individual the freedom to fulfill his own purposes . . . to achieve a place commensurate with his talents." As Bell elaborates, ". . . equality of opportunity denies . . . any . . . criterion which allocates place, other than fair competition open equally to talent and ambition . . . [it] is . . . the principle of individual merit generalized as a categorical imperative."[7] Proponents of meritocracy argue that allocating places is fair only when the most meritorious are chosen. Equal opportunity treats individuals as "choosers and doers" and "rational agents"; the individual's will to accomplish his or her goals is a paramount right, and the "most skilled" are the most rational choices to be selected.[8]

But such perspectives are challenged by alternative conceptions of qualifications, merit and desert. Walzer challenges the moral-practical justification for hiring or admitting the "best qualified": "Even if one believed in choosing the one deserving or meritorious (or 'best deserving' or most meritorious) person from out of the mass, there would be no way of identifying that person. The members of the selection committee would disagree about the appropriate balance of strengths and weaknesses, and they would disagree about the actual balance in any given individual."[9] Walzer does not argue that *anyone* is qualified for any position, but claims that it is impossible to objectively rank-order those who are qualified; there is no "best qualified". In Walzer's view, these determinations proceed from democratic establishments of the social purposes of specific positions. Such determinations can not, rationally, suspend the necessary skill requirements of a specific job, suggested by social purposes, but Walzer argues that all of the qualified are equally qualified.

Gertrude Ezorsky likewise argues that a rank-ordering of job candidates is possible but is not "a moral guide" for selection. Ezorsky claims that "basically-qualified" candidates, while not the "best qualified," can improve their skills on the job.[10] Ezorsky believes that hiring such candidates provides moral redress for social groups who suffer discrimination. Herein, she qualified classical liberal views of equal opportunity. Ezorsky implies that such alternative interpretations of merit foster equal opportunity better than do 'best qualified as most deserving' approaches.

Whereas both Walzer and Ezorsky acknowledge that some qualifications are relevant for specific positions, Iris Marion Young claims that such determinations can not be objective. Young argues: ". . . though the merit principle requires impartial technical definition of qualifications, the criteria used to determine qualifications tend to embody . . . particular values, norms, and cultural attributes. . . ." Young believes these determinations are unavoidably based on cultural and institutional biases.[11] A qualified job candidate, therefore, is only so according to a particular ideology; an elementary school teacher who instills meekness in her students in a competitive culture may be judged unqualified. Young does not deny that a rank-ordering of job candidates is rationally possible, but she deems it ideological. For Young, the crucial issue is the *nature* of the ideology. She links qualifications with social purposes; social purposes should promote democratic values, specifically, the undermining of "oppression."

Sher justifies the hiring of the "best qualified" because it respects the will and choice of rational actors, and because he believes they will perform better. Both reasons, it can be argued, serve social purposes. However, alternative views redefine social purposes. Young believes that qualifications should reflect the overcoming of oppression—entrenched societal biases that serve to limit the quality of life of particular social groups. Ronald Dworkin likewise argues that race is sometimes a valid qualification because it serves social purposes: "If a black skin will . . . enable another doctor to do a different medical job better, then a black skin is . . . merit."[12] Dworkin views race as a qualification because its use can provide role models for black youth, and because increased black participation in the professions breaks down hurtful racial stereotypes.[13]

But redefining the social purposes of qualifications requires redefining a qualification itself. This task requires a distinction between qualification and desert. As Walzer states, "*Desert* implies a very strict sort of entitlement, such that the title precedes and determines the selection, while *qualifications* is a much looser idea."[14] Walzer views desert as leaving less room for deliberation because it involves a past performance. Juries decide if someone *deserves* a particular verdict or a prize based on past behavior or performance. Selection committees, on the other hand, choose candidates according to ". . . an ongoing process of political or professional definition," regarding relevant qualifications.[15] Selection committees make judgments based on evolving institutional and public goals or purposes. The judgments are predictions about future performances, and therefore cannot be *deserved* since nothing has been performed. A doctor may be qualified, but is not *entitled* to a particular medical job. The doctor chosen for the particular job is not *entitled* to it either, but was chosen because he or she fit the bill of relevant qualifications based on current institutional and public purposes. The qualified candidates *deserve* equal consideration, but nothing more.[16] Walzer's distinction between desert and qualification lays a foundation for alternative views of merit to redefine or extend the content of 'social purposes'. If qualified candidates do not *deserve* any positions, then 'social purposes' can be viewed in nontraditional ways. Social purposes, as explicated by Sher, involve competent performances and respect for individual rational acts. In this view, choosing the "best qualified" underscores for society the moral basis of desert; the act of choosing the most deserving fulfills both social purposes. However, Walzer's distinction eliminates desert from selection processes, and opens them to other social purposes, such as the elimination of racism. For Sher, the selection decision is pre-determined by who is the most deserving; no room is left for non-traditional social purposes, and selection committees are rigidly guided by desert. Walzer's view, on the other hand, opens up the possibility of alternative and dynamic selection criteria.

Alternative views of qualifications question the objectivity and fairness of traditional methods of recruitment and selection. Traditional views of merit assume that these methods are objective. Sher's criterion of, "best qualified" as most deserving neglects to discuss how rank-orderings are determined. Sher requires that candidates be ". . . suitably skilled . . .,"[17] but does not analyze how skill is determined. Similarly, Bell's definition of meritocracy assumes that the ". . . fair competition open equally to talent and ambition. . ." *is* fair.[18] Young questions the objectivity of educational attainment and tests: "Educational attainment and test results are no more neutral than more direct evaluations of performance."[19] For Young, educational credentials and test scores are normatively and culturally biased; all methods of selection reflect ideologies which oppress some social groups, and some tests do not measure competence.[20] Ezorsky questions the fairness of traditional recruitment methods: ". . . blacks have been outside the channels leading to well-paid jobs controlled by white referral unions that recruit by word of mouth" and ". . . adverse effect on blacks is exacerbated when suburban employers rely on 'walk-in' applicants from white neighborhoods."[21]

Questioning traditional selection methods implicitly questions classical liberal notions of equal opportunity, which protect against intentional discrimination, but do *not* protect against indirect or unintentional discrimination. Tests deliberately devised to keep African-Americans out of a company are violations of classical liberal notions of equal opportunity. Invalidated tests used to distinguish qualified from unqualified or less qualified candidates, which screen out many more African-Americans than whites, are not discriminatory under this view of equal opportunity, but are the legitimate exercise of institutional freedom. Young and Ezorsky view this interpretation of equal opportunity as unfair because individuals may be screened out of competition *unfairly* or may not have the same access to the competitive pool as others.

Affirmative action is one tool used by African-Americans to attempt to achieve access to economic power and the social respect accorded to other Americans. However, affirmative action programs—in themselves—tend to reinforce the liberal values of competitive marketplace individualism, and thereby discourage the mobilization of a political force that calls for a more progressive democratic change. By helping to create a larger black middle class, affirmative action can inadvertently foster conservatism. Middle-class African-Americans may like the American competitive system or not believe that it needs much change as a result of their own relatively good socioeconomic position. Such a perspective may give sanction to the "merits" of ordinal ranking and the consignment of individual fate, solely, to the individual. Economic satisfaction may ideologically co-opt, in short, the formerly oppressed. Ideological co-opting occurs, in this case, when formerly progressive citizens accede to dominant beliefs, or when they do not struggle against or rebuke them. Although liberal policies such as affirmative action try to ameliorate disadvantage, they can also quell democratic impulses, which call for facilitating equal opportunity through universal social welfare programs.

Affirmative action is a second-best policy, in one sense, because it tries to compensate for the symptoms of inequality. Affirmative action attempts to discern potential not evident through the use of conventional indicators. But if *all* Americans had access to good education, effective health care, safe streets, and fair wages, then the symptoms of disadvantage, poorer academic performance, and the lack of both vital cultural knowledge and job networks would be decreased. Affirmative action, therefore, would have less work to do—if still necessary as a safeguard against racial discrimination.

Despite affirmative action's conservatizing tendencies and its second-best status as compared to universal programs, affirmative action policies do create better opportunities for disadvantaged racial minorities. Until American society and its public policies reflect the belief that the first priority of a just society is the elimination of destructive, socially determined inequalities, affirmative action will remain necessary.

Adding disadvantaged whites and Asians to the affirmative action pool has the potential to facilitate effective universal social welfare policies. A coalition of the lower and working-classes of all races, recognizing the right to a decent quality of life, could pursue effectively the goal of economic justice. Adding a class component to affirmative action may add, as a needed start, "class disadvantage" to the political lexicon.

NOTES

1. George Sher, Qualifications, Fairness, and Desert, in *Equal Opportunity* edited by Norman E. Bowie (Boulder, Colo.: Westview Press, 1988), p. 119

2. Michael Walzer, In Defense of Equality, *Dissent*, 20, 1973: 407.

3. Sher, "Qualifications, Fairness, and Desert", pp. 119–125.

4. Terry Eastland, *Ending Affirmative Action* (New York: Basic Books, 1996), p. 12.

5. Sher, "Qualifications, Fairness, and Desert", p. 123.

6. Daniel Bell, "On Meritocracy and Equality", *The Public Interest*, 29 (Fall 1972): 42, 30.

7. Ibid., pp. 40–41.

8. Sher, "Qualifications, Fairness, and Desert", pp. 123–124.

9. Michael Walzer, *Spheres of Justice* (New York: Basic Books, 1983), pp. 142–143.

10. Gertrude Ezorsky, *Racism and Justice* (Ithaca, New York: Cornell University Press, 1991), pp. 40–44.

11. Iris Marion Young, *Justice and the Politics of Difference* (Princeton, New Jersey: Princeton University Press, 1990), p. 204

12. Ronald Dworkin, "Are Quotas Unfair?", in *Racial Preference and Racial Justice*, edited by Russell Nieli (Washington, D.C.: Ethics and Public Policy Center, 1991), p. 185.

13. Ibid., p. 179.

14. Walzer, *Spheres of Justice*, p. 136.

15. Ibid, pp. 136–139.

16. Ibid.

17. Sher, "Qualifications, Fairness, and Desert", p. 119.

18. Bell, "On Meritocracy and Equality", p. 41.

19. Young, *Justice and the Politics of Difference*, p. 206.

20. Ibid., pp. 207–210.

21. Ezorsky, pp. 15–16.

Chapter One

Affirmative Action Policy History

ORIGINS

Affirmative action policies arose from African-Americans' struggle for citizenship in a society which has a long history of racism. Citizenship implies equal access to material comfort and social respect. While most policy histories of affirmative action designate President John F. Kennedy's Executive Order 10925 and/or Lyndon Johnson's Executive Order 11246 as the origins of affirmative action, the policy would not have been born without persistent African-American agency. The civil rights struggles of the 1950s and 1960s created a political and social context that spurred governmental attempts to give blacks equal access to employment, education, public facilities, and private institutions. Without the continuous agitation of blacks, it is difficult to comprehend the end of Jim Crow laws and the physical intimidation used to prevent blacks from voting, or the emergence of anti-discrimination efforts and affirmative action policies. Historian Mary Frances Berry points out that Arkansas' resistance to desegregating its public schools prompted ". . . the first occasion in American history when federal troops were used to enforce a federal court order favorable to blacks."[1] It was the tactics of the civil rights movement–sit-ins, marches, and boycotts–that called attention to racial inequality, yielding the 1954 Supreme Court decision, Brown vs. Board of Education, that desegregated public schools, spawning Arkansas' desegregation attempts.[2] Berry argues that black resistance to racism has often been strongly opposed with both legal and extra-legal, and violent and non-violent, tactics.[3] However, African-Americans have always persevered in their struggle for equal access to the American dream.

1

African-Americans have used electoral power, non-violent protest, and violent uprisings to attempt to achieve American citizenship for themselves. Affirmative action defender Albert G. Mosely states, ". . . [in] the mid-1950s, blacks initiated an era of non-violent direct action to publicly protest unjust laws and practices that supported racial discrimination."[4] Such agency changed public opinion and as a consequence, influenced the American government to enact pro-civil rights laws. Political sociologist Paul Burstein contends that the civil rights movement made political elites more aware of an increasingly supportive pro-civil rights public, and that violent resistance to desegregation made civil rights a salient public issue.[5] This context inspired Presidential candidate John F. Kennedy, in 1960, to ". . . [speak] more frequently and [when President, act] more sensitively on civil rights than any previous major party nominee."[6] African-Americans voted nearly seventy percent for Kennedy in the 1960 presidential election and turned out heavily in crucial Northern cities.[7] Black support for Kennedy was influenced by the National Association for the Advancement of Colored People (NAACP) and other prominent blacks' endorsements.[8] Kennedy's desire to maintain favor among African-Americans, but not alienate congressional Dixiecrats nor southern voters, resulted in his signing Executive Order 10925, which began affirmative action in lieu of major civil rights legislation. Kennedy's motivation went beyond electoral concerns, also addressing America's image among foreign nations. According to Carl Brauer, the Kennedy administration sought to impress foreign diplomats by reciting its efforts to end employment discrimination.[9] Both of the administration's reasons for initiating affirmative action, which in 1961 meant attempting to diversify the applicant pool, especially in federal government jobs, and to hire more blacks in such positions and in business as with federal contracts, were a result of blacks using their electoral power and the great civil rights marches, protests, and boycotts of the 1950s and 1960s.

The words "affirmative action" were first used in connection with civil rights policy in 1961, in President John F. Kennedy's Executive Order 10925. This order was established to promote and ensure non-discrimination in government employment and in the employment practices of government contractors and sub-contractors. The term "affirmative action" appeared in reference to government contractors: "The contractor will take affirmative action to ensure that applicants are employed and that employees are treated during employment without regard to their race, creed, color or national origin."[10] Executive Order 10925 established the President's Committee on Equal Employment Opportunity (PCEEO) to enforce nondiscrimination by conducting compliance reviews and imposing sanctions where warranted. The word "qualified" appears in the beginning of the order: ". . . to promote and ensure equal opportunity for all qualified persons . . ." and ". . . to encourage by positive measures equal opportunity for all qualified persons . . ."[11]

What did Executive Order 10925 mean in actual practice? In 1961, PCEEO's surveys of federal government employment found that African-American employment in middle and higher level civil service jobs was dramatically small.[12] During the Kennedy administration, the percentages of blacks in craft, professional, and administrative jobs, in the private sector, remained extremely low.[13] In federal government employment, the Kennedy administration's efforts produced some improvement; by 1963 blacks held 13.1 percent of federal jobs.[14] However, Kennedy was still affirming the need for affirmative action in late 1963.[15]

Lyndon Johnson issued Executive Order 11246 in 1965. Johnson had served as chairman of PCEEO and believed that the federal government needed to enforce non-discrimination. Johnson's speech at Howard University, in June 1965, implied that government had to take an active role to ensure equal opportunity: "For the task is to give 20 million Negroes the same chance as every other American to . . . work and . . . to develop their ability."[16] However, Executive Order 11246 did not require hiring or promotion goals. Executive Order 11246 was very similar to Executive Order 10925 except for its creation of the Office of Federal Contract Compliance (OFCC) in the Department of Labor. E.O. 11246 also transferred PCEEO's function of ensuring non-discrimination in federal government employment to the Civil Service Commission. Ensurance of non-discrimination in federal government contracts was re-assigned from PCEEO to OFCC.[17] PCEEO's efforts in the private sector, regarding the non-discrimination commitments of businesses and reports of minority employment and promotion progress, became the province of the Equal Employment Opportunity Commission (EEOC). EEOC was created by the Civil Rights Act of 1964 to enforce non-discrimination in private employment.[18]

What did Executive Order 11246 and EEOC efforts look like in practice? OFCC had the power to impose sanctions on federal contractors who did not comply with the executive order. This meant that companies who were found to have discriminated against minorities could lose current and future federal government contracts. The United States Commission on Civil Rights reported in 1969 that despite numerous findings of non-compliance by the Commission, OFCC had rarely imposed suits, recommendations for suits, or contract debarments. Not one contract had been canceled; only two contractors were sued or recommended for suit; and only one hearing to investigate non-compliance was held.[19] In the mid-to-late 1960s, EEOC did not have the power to file discrimination suits but could only attempt to eliminate discrimination by persuasion, conference, or conciliation. In 1966 EEOC began gathering data on businesses' racial employment patterns through the use of the EEO-1 form. In 1966 EEOC published the results of a large national survey on job patterns for minorities and women in private industry. EEOC concluded that employment discrimination was widespread in almost every occupational group and industry. One of the major findings of the study was the large concentration of minority employees in lower-paying occupations and their under-representation in higher paying ones.[20] In 1969 the United States Commission on Civil Rights reported that the EEOC had not been very successful in getting more minorities into higher-paid positions, even in companies from four major cities, where EEOC held investigative hearings.[21] A 1969 report, commissioned by the United States Commission on Civil Rights, claimed that the EEOC had barely improved the job position of minorities in its first thirty-two months of existence.[22] However, Nixon administration efforts to speed up the hiring of African-Americans resulted in making such efforts a hot-button issue up to the present time. However, six years prior to Nixon's actions some political elites were expressing concern about merit in the context of equal opportunity efforts.

THE COLLISION OF TRADITIONAL AND ALTERNATIVE CONCEPTIONS OF FAIRNESS

The desire to assure equal opportunity and reward merit motivated congressional debate during the passage of the Civil Rights Act of 1964. The Illinois Fair Employment Practice Commission (FEPC) overturned the Motorola Corporation's rejection of a black job applicant based on his performance on a general ability test, setting the context for the debate. The commission rejected the test as unfair to "culturally deprived and disadvantaged groups" because it did not take into account inequalities and differences in environment."[23] The hearing examiner ordered Motorola to hire the applicant *and* to cease giving the test. The Motorola case provided the impetus for a proposed amendment to the civil rights bill, which eventually became section 703(h) of Title VII of the Civil Rights Act of 1964. Section 703(h) stated that the use of a "professionally developed ability test" was legal unless it was "designed, intended or used to discriminate because of race, color, religion, sex, or national origin."[24]

   The Motorola case illuminated the issues during congressional debates of the civil rights bill that transcended congressmen's fears that the proposed bill might jeopardize test use. Some congressmen also feared that employers' freedom would be further compromised by their being forced, by the proposed EEOC, to achieve and maintain racial balances in their work forces.

Prior to the Motorola decision, Senator Lister Hill of Alabama had expressed the fear that bureaucrats might cite the proposed ban on discrimination in federally assisted programs in order to interpret racial workforce imbalances as discriminatory.[25] These concerns resulted in section 703 (j) in Title VII, which stated that racial imbalances in workforces, unless caused by discrimination, would not require employers ". . . to grant preferential treatment to any individual or group. . ."[26]

The inclusion in the Civil Rights Act of 1964 of Sections 703(h) and 703(j) reflected the concerns of some political elites that employers would be forced by the newly-created EEOC to decrease the use of traditional employment selection procedures. How did the political elite supporters of the Act respond to these concerns during the debates? Vice-President Humphrey stated: "Title VII is designed to encourage hiring on the basis of ability and qualifications, not race or religion."[27] Senator Joseph Clark of Pennsylvania and Senator Clifford Case of New Jersey put the case succinctly:

> There is no requirement in Title VII that employers abandon bona fide qualification tests where, because of differences in background and education, members of some groups are able to perform better on these tests than members of other groups. An employer may set his qualifications as high as he likes, he may test to determine which applicants have these qualifications, and he may hire, assign, and promote on the basis of test performance.[28]

All three of the bill's proponents assured critics that employers would not be encouraged, coerced or dissuaded from employing traditional selection procedures. Humphrey, Clark, and Case, in effect, argued that equal opportunity means *simply* that a job applicant's race, religion, or ethnicity cannot enter into a qualification profile. These bill proponents did not advocate the argument of the Illinois FEPC examiner: that cultural biases may have caused the racial imbalance resulting from testing, nor did they say that a test may not be related to real job qualifications. Ironically, Clark and Case seem to admit the plausibility of FEPC's positions, but then inexplicably support the use of selection methods that they imply *may* be biased.

Two Nixon administration actions, The Philadelphia Plan and Revised Order No. Four, and the Supreme Court decision in *Griggs vs Duke Power Company* (1971), provoked anti-affirmative action claims which are still lodged in 2009. The Philadelphia Plan grew out of a government survey of metropolitan Philadelphia that revealed that blacks comprised 0.5 percent of the area's plumbers and pipefitters. As a result of these findings, construction contractors in metropolitan Philadelphia were required to submit pre-award hiring goals for minorities. The goals were based on the percentage of blacks in the metropolitan Philadelphia labor force.[29] Revised Order No. Four required all government contractors holding contracts of $50,000 or more, to file affirmative action programs with OFCC within four months of contract award. Contractors were required to analyze their employment patterns by race, and to establish goals with timetables if underutilizations were found. Underutilization meant ". . . having fewer minorities in a particular job group than would reasonably be expected by their availability." Determining underutilization meant considering "the general availability of minorities having requisite skills in an area in which the contractor can reasonably recruit."[30] OFCC could cease doing future business with contractors who did not ". . . show good cause for . . . failure to [comply] . . ."[31]

Both OFCC actions provoked opposition in Congress, and from organized labor. The AFL-CIO opposed the Philadelphia Plan and the Contractors Association of Eastern Pennsylvania sued the Secretary of Labor over it. Senate opponents, calling the Plan "Preferential hiring of persons on the basis of race . . ." and ". . . discrimination in reverse . . .," proposed a rider intended to deny funding to any contract found by the General Accounting Office (GAO) to violate federal contract law. GAO opposed the Philadelphia Plan, believing that it violated federal contract law. The rider passed the Senate but was defeated in the House because of strenuous pro-Plan efforts by the Nixon administration.[32] Senator Sam Ervin of North Carolina, referring to Revised Order No. Four as making minority hiring ". . . flatly mandatory," proposed an anti-quota amendment to the Equal Employment Opportunity Act of 1972.[33] The amendment was defeated, but the debate over it set the terms of debate over affirmative action for years to come. Those who opposed the Philadelphia Plan and Revised Order No. Four made frequent use of the language of reverse discrimination, proportional representation, and quotas. Into the 21st century, affirmative action remains a highly charged and hotly-debated issue.[34]

Griggs ruled as discriminatory ". . . an employment practice which operates to exclude Negroes [if it] . . . cannot be shown to be related to job performance . . ."[35] *Griggs* proscribes "practices that are fair in form, but discriminatory in operation."[36] An employment test that screens out job applicants is discriminatory if the test does not measure requisite skills. The *Griggs* ruling is linked by policy critics with demands for proportional racial representation in employment and the hire of unqualified and less qualified minorities.[37] Affirmative action critics claim that the Philadelphia Plan, Revised Order No. Four, and *Griggs* signaled a sea-change in the policy goal from equality of opportunity to proportional representation, which, they claim, runs roughshod over hiring by merit. Political and public controversy over affirmative action, provoked by these 1969–71 events reached a fever pitch in the Supreme Court decision in *Regents of the University of California vs Bakke* (1978). How has affirmative action been defended?

THE POLITICAL DEFENSES OF AFFIRMATIVE ACTION AND THEIR LIMITS

The Supreme Court defended affirmative action in *Bakke*, but it is important to first look at prior justifications for the policy. The inclusion in the Civil Rights Act of 1964 of Section 706(g) arose from congressional concerns that unintentional discrimination would be subject, under the Act, to government action. Section 706(g) states that discrimination occurs only if employers intend to discriminate. Humphrey assured the Congress that ". . . inadvertent or accidental discrimination will not violate the title . . ."[38] 706(g) reminded employers, as did 703(h), that selection devices that unintentionally exclude African-Americans from candidate pools, such as tests, were still legal. The civil rights bill debates, in failing to discuss test effects and relevance, protracted the missing discussions of appropriate qualifications among politically elite definitions of equal opportunity that had first been notable in the Kennedy administration. Executive Order 10925 stated, without explanation of the word "qualified" that ". . . it is the plain . . . obligation of the United States Government to promote and ensure equal opportunity for all qualified persons . . ."[39] Interestingly, though, without explanation, the order also asked executive departments and agencies to provide recommendations ". . . for the elimination of any discrimination, direct and indirect, which now exists."[40] These references in E.O. 10925 to "qualified" and "indirect discrimination" remained unexplained in a statement Kennedy made near the end of his administration: "I do think that we ought to make an effort to give fair chance to everyone who is qualified . . ."[41] According to Business Council chairman Frederic Kappel, a meeting between Kennedy and the Business Council in 1963, regarding the administration's approach to affirmative action, gave the impression that ". . . [Kennedy] felt that in some circumstances business would be justified in going out and finding Negroes in order to get programs started and established."[42] This statement, like the reference to "qualified" in E.O. 10925, suggest that the early architects of affirmative action accepted the validity of traditional notions of "qualifications" since it had not been debated anywhere. The vague reference in E.O. 10925 to "indirect discrimination" suggests, as did the Clark and Case statement, that traditional selection procedures may be worth analyzing for their relevance and discriminatory effect, but neither Kennedy nor Clark and Case took this further.

The depiction of equal opportunity in early discussions of affirmative action policy suggests that even though the original policy was more assertive than the critical literature has argued,[43] traditional notions of merit remained unchallenged. Kennedy clearly believed that affirmative action would lead to the frequent *hiring* of African-Americans, not just to the expansion or integration of candidate pools. As Carl Brauer points out, "Kennedy . . . observed that businessmen contemplating establishing operations in the South could be particularly helpful by hiring Negroes."[44] Despite this more assertive approach to affirmative action, Kennedy's insistence that the hired be "qualified", without explication of the term, suggests that equal opportunity meant finding African-Americans who did well on employment tests and had the required academic degrees. Kennedy initiated a non-traditional approach to equal opportunity, targeting members of an oppressed group for jobs, but he believed in what John Skrentny calls "the abstract individual model." According to Skrentny, Americans have always believed that ". . . one deserved all that one could attain by talent and industry."[45] The purpose of government according to this view is to maintain a situation in which the individual could pursue his or her goals by making use of his or her talents and industry with as few fetters as possible, with those talents judged by objective criteria.[46] Equal opportunity as depicted here is the right to *pursue* individually determined wants, but the outcomes of such pursuits are something beyond the proper role of government regulation or intervention. According to this view, the determiner of outcomes is merit, as defined by employers. However, the threat of cultural biases, subjectively determined relevant qualifications, and indirect discrimination–hinted at but then dropped by Kennedy, Clark, and Case–locate a possible vulnerability in this depiction of equal opportunity. The abstract individual model assumes the objectivity of selection criteria and an inherent fairness in results presuming that everyone has the opportunity to pursue his or her economic and material goals. The freedom of employers, as affirmed by the Civil Rights Act of 1964, to use selection devices of their choice may not produce results that are fair *even if* the same selection devices that are used for all applicants and employers do not intentionally discriminate.

What arguments had pro-plan actors used in the battle over the Philadelphia Plan? The Nixon administration justified the Philadelphia Plan by arguing that it redressed the effects of past discrimination against African-Americans. Nixon's Secretary of Labor, George Schultz, decried the "appalling unemployment experience of black teen-agers." Schultz argued that African-Americans had been excluded from word-of-mouth job information and hinted that non-traditional approaches to remedy the effects of economic marginalization might be beneficial.[47] Arthur Fletcher, Schultz' Assistant Secretary for Wage and Labor Standards, justified the plan's goals and timetables as necessary to ". . . correct obvious imbalances . . ." in the racial make-ups of construction company workforces.[48] Jerris Leonard, the Nixon Department of Justice's Assistant Attorney General for Civil Rights, described the plan as an attempt to help African-Americans "catch up" in obtaining construction jobs, from which they had been largely shut out.[49] Fletcher and Leonard used craft-union membership statistics to argue that African-Americans had been discriminated against in the past.[50] Taken together, Schultz, Leonard, and Fletcher justified the controversial Philadelphia Plan and its non-traditional uses of goals and timetables on the grounds that past discrimination created the "obvious imbalances" and exclusions from informal job information networks. These political elites implied that a conception of equal opportunity as simply non-discrimination laws would not significantly improve racial imbalances. In order to promote equal opportunity, contractors, they suggested, must aggressively recruit, train, and hire blacks. Leonard implied that construction skills could be learned through apprenticeships; blacks, largely inexperienced in these trades due to discrimination, were to be hired. But again the issue of relevant qualifications did not become the focus of the affirmative action defense. Philadelphia Plan defenders, ignoring merit issues, justified the plan on the grounds of past discrimination.

The Philadelphia Plan defenders could have argued that the skilled craft jobs, for which the plan targeted minorities, had been, and still were, shut out.[51] The plan intended to get construction companies to hire black apprentices, as well as skilled black craftsmen. Defenders could have pointed out that the plan's minority hiring goals did not require selecting the unqualified or less qualified; black apprentices would become skilled on the job–as had white skilled craftsmen. Such a defense has powerful implications for the affirmative action debate. Some jobs require minimal qualifications, but becoming skilled at them takes practice. Apprentice carpenters must demonstrate, by the end of their apprenticeship, skill at cutting, measuring, and tool-handling, among other things, which suggests to employers that they have the necessary knowledge and skill that experience will increase. For jobs that require minimal qualifications, many applicants are often equally qualified; one "best" candidate is non-existent.[52] In such cases, rank ordering applicants is meaningless, and hiring an equally qualified African-American to increase diversity and ensure fairness cannot be discriminatory. All of the qualified candidates have the necessary entry-level qualifications, and practice will increase their skills. A general aptitude test used for selecting among successful apprentice carpenters is irrelevant for discerning their carpentry skills, and is discriminatory if it screens out those who got low scores. Since blacks, on average, do worse than whites on general aptitude tests[53], such tests must be valid and accurately discern those who will perform well from those who will not on the jobs the tests are administered for. These arguments were not used by affirmative action defenders.

A justification of affirmative action that relies on past discrimination and does not debunk merit is vulnerable to the premises of Skrentny's abstract individual model of American political culture. As Skrentny points out, Americans tend to believe "the land of opportunity was . . . meritocratic; one deserved all that one could attain by talent and industry."[54] A public policy that implements race-based hiring goals justified by the existence of *past* discrimination strikes many Americans as compensation for inequities of the past, resulting in non-merit based hiring and admitting. If discrimination is mainly a thing of the past, as the defense of the Philadelphia Plan appears to say, why would hiring goals need to be implemented? The American individualist who merely wants government to ensure a level-playing field and who believes that discrimination is a phenomenon of the past, presumes that equal opportunity is already assured. This same American, accordingly, views racial hiring goals as compensation for past injustices that produces hiring based not on "talent and industry", but, as Jerris Leonard stated, ". . . catching up . . ."[55] The individualist views civil society as if it should contain only one guarantee: a level playing field. According to this model, a hiring goal intended to help formerly excluded groups catch up signals unjust guarantees and violates the level playing field sanctioned by equal opportunity. An affirmative action defense that relies solely on claims of past discrimination is vulnerable in a political culture which presumes that equal opportunity already exists.

Some political elite defenders of the Philadelphia Plan did allude to the issue of qualifications. Schulz stated that "hiring standards and actual job requirements" might not match.[56] Similarly, Attorney General John Mitchell said, "The obligation of non-discrimination . . . in some circumstances may not permit . . . indifference to the racial consequences of alternative courses of action which involve the application of outwardly neutral criteria."[57] Both Mitchell and Schulz alluded to a questioning of traditional qualification criteria. Their allusions, however, did not elicit further discussion from the Nixon administration and remained peripheral to the political elites' "past discrimination defense" of the Philadelphia Plan.

The 1971 Supreme Court case *Griggs vs Duke Power Company* took up a point that had been the focus of the Motorola case. The Motorola case revolved around the use of employment tests as legitimate or illegitimate selection methods for "culturally deprived and disadvantaged groups" because the Motorola test did not account for "inequalities and differences in environment"[58] The Illinois FEPC, which objected to the rejection of a black applicant who had performed below the required standard on the test, based its decision on the grounds that the test was biased against African-Americans. The implication in FEPC's argument was that the test did not accurately locate those who have or do not have the ability to successfully perform the specific job(s).

Griggs revolved around the use of two employment tests administered by the Duke Power Company of North Carolina. Duke Power's requirements of a passing score on both tests and a high school diploma as conditions for employment and transfer were challenged by thirteen African-American Duke Power employees. These requirements did not intend to measure the ability to perform a particular job or category of jobs, but Duke Power believed they "generally improve[d] the overall quality of the workforce."[59] The Supreme Court ruled that the poorer scores and lower number of high school diplomas among Duke Power's African-American employees relative to whites "would appear to be directly traceable to race." The Court elaborated: "Basic intelligence must have the means of articulation to manifest itself fairly in a testing process. Because they are Negroes, petitioners have long received inferior education . . ."[60] This implied that possessing knowledge and the means to articulate it in a written test may be distinct processes. A testee could *know* what a test question asked for, but not be able to express this knowledge in writing, or answer it in a specific test format. The Court implied that the "inferior education" African-Americans had received in the South precluded them from performing well on the tests. But the major thrust of *Griggs* is that what the Duke Power tests tested was irrelevant to job performance. According to Griggs, ". . . neither the high school completion requirement nor the general intelligence test is shown to bear a demonstrable relationship to successful performance of the jobs for which it was used . . .", and "[t]he evidence shows that employees who have not completed high school or taken the tests have continued to perform satisfactorily and make progress in departments for which the high school and test criteria are now used."[61] The Court argued that employment tests and diplomas are not legitimate parts of a selection process if they screen out job applicants who *can* perform the specific job(s). This Supreme Court argument has been overlooked by political defenders of affirmative action. By doing so, defenders refrain from asking critics of affirmative action the reasonable question, "Does a particular selection device do what the user claims it does?" If it does not, according to *Griggs*, then it is ". . . discriminatory in operation."[62] The American public did not get to hear the rational view of qualifications that *Griggs* argues since the case was not specifically about affirmative action and did not command the public's attention. By contrast the *Bakke* case was the first national lightening-rod moment for affirmative action.

Bakke: Missed Opportunity for Discourse

The 1978 Supreme Court case, *Regents of the University of California vs Bakke*, was the first public moment in the history of affirmative action.[63] *Bakke* made public the frequent controversy around the policy in private, political[64] and academic circles.[65] The case itself dealt only with a minority admissions set-aside plan at the University of California at Davis, but judging from the unusual amount of attention it generated[66], the case's merits were now eclipsed. The media and public viewed the case as a test of "reverse discrimination," "quotas," and "preferential treatment."[67]

Alan Bakke sued the University of California at Davis' Medical School on grounds that he had been denied admission to the medical school because of race. The suit pointed out that Bakke had higher test scores and grade point average than did minority students who were admitted to the Medical School under Davis' set-aside program. The Davis Medical School set-aside program reserved sixteen places annually for minority students. By the time Bakke's application was processed, the only places left were reserved for minority students.[68]

The Supreme Court ruled that the Davis affirmative action program was unconstitutional on grounds that it disregarded the individual right to equal protection of the laws.[69] According to the Court, Bakke had not personally discriminated against minorities but had been made, under Davis' program, to bear the burden of remedying ". . . societal discrimination . . ."[70] However, the Court also ruled that ". . . a properly devised admissions program . . ."[71] could take race into account as one factor in overall admissions decisions, in order to promote a diverse student body. The opinion fortified this by stating: "It is not too much to say that the nation's future depends upon leaders trained through wide exposure to the ideas and mores of students as diverse as this Nation of many peoples."[72] The opinion alluded to the need for cultural awareness in the training of doctors: "[P]hysicians serve a heterogeneous population;" therefore, the exposure of medical students to ". . . medicine experiences, outlooks and ideas . . ."from various backgrounds is ". . . a constitutionally permissible goal for an institution of higher education."[73] The Court qualified its defense of racial consideration in college admissions programs by declaring that race could not be the sole determinant of admission, but it could be considered one legitimate factor in an individual's mix of ". . . combined qualifications . . ."[74] In other words, the *Bakke* opinion sanctions the addition of race and ethnic background to the traditional mix of qualifications. In so doing, the opinion affirms such traditional qualifications as test scores, grade point averages, state residency, family history, or relatives who graduated from Davis. Therefore, the opinion evades any discussion of the *Griggs* argument; though Griggs dealt with employment, college admissions is fair territory for assessing the legitimacy of qualification.

The *Bakke* defense of racial consideration in college admissions leaves intact the assumed objectivity and validity of traditional selection methods. While the *Bakke* opinion expands the parameters of these methods by adding racial and ethnic considerations, it does not analyze the objectivity or validity of test scores or grade point averages. The Court's only reference to traditional selection methods appears to support its assumed objectivity. The opinion refers to racial and ethnic considerations as ". . . nonobjective factors . . ."[75] This implies that other factors such as test scores and grade point averages are objective factors. Other than this oblique reference, the *Bakke* opinion does not analyze traditional academic selection criteria.

Using racial and ethnic diversity as the central defense of affirmative action without a clear analysis of merit cannot weaken the American preference for individual achievement.[76] The diversity argument remains weak for many Americans because they perceive that diversity can only justly be sanctioned by individual industry. According to this perspective, if individuals of various backgrounds apply themselves vigorously to the goal of medical school admission, diversity should be achieved. A program designed to achieve diversity is, therefore, unnecessary and would be unfair because it provided advantage based on race. The entrenchment of belief in individual competition for life goals can better be challenged if defenders of affirmative action can show that certain societal groups are discriminated against by standard "competitive" rules, as *Griggs* implies. If they fail to show this form of present discrimination, the Court's argument on behalf of diversity because it promotes ". . . a robust exchange of ideas . . ."[77] does not effectively counter protests of "merit violations." Diversity appears, to many Americans, to ignore merit; these Americans perceive that the goal of increased minority representation in colleges runs roughshod over desert.

The diversity justification, without *Griggs*-like analysis of merit cannot tackle the prevailing individualism amongst a white majority who ". . . do not see themselves as racists or as opponents of equal opportunity . . ."[78], yet oppose affirmative action on merit grounds. The *Bakke* opinion depicts a view of equal opportunity that is essentially in keeping with the ideology of individualism. The emphasis on diversity, without a clear analysis of the inordinate power given to traditional selection procedures, indicates that equal opportunity did not concern the Court majority in *Bakke*. *Bakke's* central thrust—that cultural diversity is enriching to the educational environment—expands traditional concepts of qualifications, but there is no discussion by the Court of the relationship of present discrimination to traditional concepts of merit and equal opportunity. Unlike *Griggs*, the *Bakke* opinion does not explain that no single criteria should be controlling. A defense disembodied from such intellectually powerful underpinnings meant that the public in the late 1970s heard a relatively weak and unconvincing defense of affirmative action. Those propagating the ideology of individualism walk away from *Bakke* having heard little cogent challenge to the belief that equal opportunity is pervasive in today's society.

Sea-Change and the Continuing Battle

The 1989 Supreme Court Case *Ward's Cove Packing Company vs Antonio* signifies the beginning of a sea-change in the Supreme Court's attitude toward affirmative action.[79] This shift by the Court was the culmination of efforts by the Reagan administrations to dramatically roll back affirmative action. The administration appointed three Supreme Court justices who were critical of affirmative action.[80] The *Wards Cove* decision made the *Griggs* argument–that discrimination can be practiced unintentionally through unfair selection procedures–harder to prove. The *Griggs* decision had put the burden of proof on employers to show that their selection procedures, if challenged as discriminatory, were a necessity for the successful running of their businesses. The *Wards Cove* ruling put the burden of proving discrimination on the applicant or employee. Under *Griggs*, the plaintiff could prove discrimination by showing that a company had a statistical racial imbalance in its workforce,[81] but under *Wards Cove* the employees or applicants had ". . . to demonstrate that the disparity they complain of is the result of one or more of the employment practices that they are attacking . . ."[82] In addition to making discrimination harder to prove, *Wards Cove* also lessened the employer's burden of having to justify a selection procedure that led to disproportionately small numbers of minority hirings. According to *Wards Cove*, the new standard for business justification was ". . . whether a challenged practice serves, in a significant way, the legitimate employment goals of the employer." Wards Cove read the Griggs standard to mean ". . . essential or indispensable to the employer's business . . ."which it saw as ". . . almost impossible for most employers to meet . . ."[83]

The *Wards Cove* decision rested upon traditionalist notions of employer freedom and merit. Non-white Wards Cove Company employees, the original plaintiffs, had charged that the Wards Cove hiring and promoting practices caused a racial stratification in the work force. The Supreme Court ruled that this charge was based on an improper statistical comparison because it had been made between the Wards Cove Cannery and noncannery jobs, but not between ". . . the racial composition of the at issue jobs and the racial composition of the qualified population in the relevant labor market."[84] The opinion implied that the relevant issue is not racial work-force statistical differences in general, but only those specific to the pool of those "qualified" for the cannery jobs. According to the Court, discrimination findings based solely on companies' racial work-force profiles ignore qualifications and may lead an employer to ". . . adopt racial quotas, insuring that no portion of his work force deviates from the other portions . . ."[85] Plaintiffs who demonstrated that the test used by a business caused a disproportionate percentage of blacks to be eliminated from hiring pools had the burden of proving discrimination if the test served ". . . the legitimate employment goals of the employer . . ."[86] A "business necessity" justification was no longer the standard. Business necessity meant, according to *Griggs*, that tests ". . . .bear a demonstrable relationship to successful performance of the jobs for which [they are] used."[87] The *Wards Cove* standard , ". . . legitimate employment goals . . .,"[88] is not defined by the Court, but, as the legislative history of the Civil Rights Act of 1991 points out, can be interpreted to permit ". . . exclusionary practices that are *not* necessary for successful job performance . . . so long as [they] . . . serve any legitimate business objective."[89] Did the Civil Rights Act of 1991, responding to *Wards Cove*, explain the parameters of legitimate qualifications?

The Civil Rights Act of 1991: Employer Prerogative or Applicant Protection?

The Civil Rights Act of 1991 attempted to respond to the *Wards Cove* ruling. The 1991 Act maintained, as had *Wards Cove*, that plaintiffs in employment discrimination cases had to prove that a specific employment practice had caused a racial exclusion. However, the Act differed from *Wards Cove* in affirming "business necessity" rather than the possibly weaker standard of "serving legitimate employer goals." While the Act's interpretive memorandum states that one of its purposes is to ". . . codify the concepts of "business necessity" and "job related"[qualifications] enunciated by the Supreme Court in *Griggs* and in other decisions prior to *Wards Cove*,"[90] other parts of the interpretive memorandum cloud this purpose of the Act. The interpretive memorandum states, ". . . [t]he bill is no longer designed to overrule the meaning of business necessity in *Wards Cove* . . . [i]nstead, the bill seeks to codify the meaning of "business necessity" in *Griggs* and other pre-*Wards Cove* cases– a meaning which is fully consistent with the use of the concept in *Wards Cove*."[91] Though these two passages appear to be contradictory, the memorandum attempts to clarify the confusion by demonstrating a similarity between *Griggs* standards and the *Wards Cove* standards. The memorandum points to the 1979 *New York City Transit Authority v. Beazer* decision as an exemplar of the Griggs standard; employment practices must bear a ". . . manifest relationship to the employment in question,"[92] which the memorandum states ". . . is identical . . ." with the evidentiary standards employers must meet in *Wards Cove*.[93] The *Beazer* decision upheld a New York Transit Authority rule that precluded drug addicts getting methadone treatment from employment. The ruling was based on the premise ". . . that [the employer's] legitimate employment goals of safety and efficiency require the exclusion of all users of illegal narcotics . . ."[94] The memorandum proposes that *Beazer* is consistent with the *Griggs* standards of business necessity and is also consistent with the *Wards Cove* standards of ". . . legitimate employment goals of the employer . . ."[95] This implies that the interpretation of 'business necessity' was not changed by *Wards Cove*. The memorandum further attempts to clarify the meaning of "business necessity" and "job related" by stating that these terms are ". . . to be read broadly, to include any legitimate business purpose, even those that may not be strictly required for the actual day-to-day activities of an entry level job."[96]

If an employer can, legally, require qualifications which are not ". . .strictly required for the actual day-to-day activities of an entry level job," then, as the legislative history of the Civil Rights Act of 1991 points out, it may be impossible for employees to prove indirect discrimination. The legislative history argues that employees cannot prove ". . . that there is *no* business justification whatsoever for an employment practice,"[97] implying that Wards Cove gave employers nearly unlimited discretion over selection criteria. However, the Act's interpretive memorandum does not explicate what ". . . strictly required . . ." means, and therefore can also be read as giving employers the freedom to establish broad parameters for qualifications, therefore eclipsing business necessity and allowing discriminatory selection criteria. An employer could require that all of his/ her unskilled workers have a high school diploma, and though this is not "strictly required" for successful job performance, the memorandum appears to legalize it. Using *Beazer* as an exemplar of the appropriate evidentiary requirement for "job related" and "business necessity" further confuses the Act's interpretation. *Beazer* noted that the exclusion of methadone users was "job related" because a significant number of methadone users were not drug-free and all were in the process of drug treatment.[98] Those treated with methadone maintenance often have long substance-abuse histories and need to be drug-free for a reasonable amount of time because recidivism is common.[99] The Transit Authority's requirement is a business necessity; workers' performance is impaired if they are working while "under the influence" and is crucial to facilitating a legitimate business goal– safety. *Beazer* is not an illustration of a qualification that is not strictly required for driving buses and subways, or maintaining transit equipment. The resulting ambiguity of legitimate qualifications in the Civil Rights Act of 1991, again, points to the need for public debate and resolution about merit.

The uncertain meaning of "business necessity" and "job related", as explained in the Civil Rights Act of 1991, provides no clear defense for affirmative action practices. The concept of unintentional discrimination argued in the *Griggs* decision and instituted in EEOC and OFCCP employment selection guidelines attempts to broaden the concepts of fairness and unfairness in the employment process by implying that present discrimination comes from traditional employment selection practices that irrationally, for no valid purpose, exclude some individual members of a social group significantly more than others. Recognizing this form of present employment discrimination is essential to the affirmative action goal of equal opportunity. Accordingly, the seminal concepts from *Griggs* need a rational, clear and consistent explication from defenders in order to serve the goal of true, substantive equal opportunity. Defenders must show that irrelevant, or not so definitive qualifications, along with present racial discrimination, fail to level the playing field for African-Americans.

Despite the attempt by Congress, in the Civil Rights Act of 1991, to interpret the meaning of discrimination in a manner favorable to affirmative action practices, conservatives have continued to try to roll back the policy. Since the 1989 *City of Richmond vs J.A. Crosson Co.* decision, which struck down a public contracts program, set-aside programs in eighteen locales have been struck down by courts.[100] In *Adarand Constructors vs Pena*, in 1995, the Supreme Court struck down a federal government sub-contracting clause that awards prime contractors a ten percent bonus if they hire "socially and economically disadvantaged" businesses.[101] *Adarand* set in motion a 2001 case, *Adarand Constructors vs Mineta*[102] and *Concrete Works of Colorado Inc. vs Denver* in 2003.[103] In both cases affirmative action programs were challenged, but federal courts upheld the programs and the Supreme Court refused or abandoned the suits. Attempts to end a federal contract set-aside program in Congress in 1998 also failed.[104] Despite these victories, California voters outlawed affirmative action in the public sector in 1996,[105] voters in the state of Washington passed a similar ban in 1998, and the state of Florida voluntarily banned race and gender considerations in college admissions and public contracts in 2000.[106] Clearly, affirmative action remains vulnerable to on-going political and electoral battles, which suggests that high-profile supporters of the policy have not produced a compelling defense. Former President Clinton's defense of affirmative action will be explored in the next section to illustrate this point.

Clinton and Proposition 209: Hollow Utterances

The Clinton administration opposed the Civil Rights Initiative (CCRI), also known as Proposition 209, which ended affirmative action in California's public sector: "Rather than mending what's wrong with affirmative action programs that exist, this proposition [Proposition 209] has the effect of abolishing affirmative action."[107] The administration tried to have Proposition 209 overturned, but a federal appeals court ruled that it was constitutional,[108] and the Supreme Court refused to hear the appeal. Clinton objected to the CCRI on the grounds that it would rapidly ". . . re-segregate higher education . . .," and as evidence,[109] he pointed to the "plummeting" minority enrollments in California state colleges since its enactment.[110] Clinton supported affirmative action because it ". . . tak[es] special measures to help disadvantaged people . . ."[111] and brings opportunities in education and employment to victims of persistent discrimination.[112] However, Clinton did not say that the disadvantages and discrimination facing blacks, in part, are unfair selection criteria. By neglecting to highlight the present discrimination that would result from traditional merit standards, as many elite proponents of affirmative action have done since its origins, Clinton's defense is not convincing to most Americans. If Clinton demonstrated that standardized tests, educational requirements, and grades, in some cases, do not necessarily identify the more qualified from the less qualified, he could have persuaded more Americans that affirmative action is just. A 1995 Gallup poll, which revealed that a forty-eight percent plurality of Americans favors hiring a well-qualified minority over an equally qualified white in businesses that have few minorities, suggests that there is room for re-conceptualizing merit in American political culture. Such a defense of affirmative action is imperative in building greater public support for the policy and thereby defeating efforts to roll it back.

Michigan: Victory and Vulnerability

In 2003, the Supreme Court ruled on two cases involving affirmative action efforts at the University of Michigan. Considering both cases, *Gratz v. Bollinger* and *Grutter v. Bollinger*, the Court was critical of the university's undergraduate admissions practice, which it said assigned too much weight to race, but the Court upheld the University of Michigan's law school practice of trying to ensure that minorities comprise 10 to 12 percent of each class.[113] The Court's defense of affirmative action in the law school was heavily grounded in the benefits of diversity justification, and because the law school practice did not assign inordinate influence to race.[114] However, as I have argued, such defenses do not seem to be compelling, as evidenced by the success of efforts to have Michigan voters ban affirmative action through a referendum initiated in November 2004.[115]

THE LIMITS OF CLASSICAL LIBERAL EQUAL OPPORTUNITY

The traditional view of equal opportunity suffers from a gross underestimation of the barriers to a level playing-field. The notion that government's role is to provide individuals with the freedom to pursue contracts ignores barriers that appear to be neutral and equalizing–standardized tests given to all job or college admissions candidates. As John Skrentny points out, Americans have traditionally believed ". . . that a social contract refereeing self-interest was all that was necessary to produce justice . . ."[116] The refereeing of self-interest does not interfere with situations in which the same employment tests are administered to *all* job applicants or employees, according to the traditional view of equal opportunity. From this view, a compelling public interest does not appear to be compromised because all are being treated equally. The lower scores of one racial group as compared to another would not appear ominous or conspicuous because the test had been fairly administered. Accordingly, no unfair barrier is perceived within the logic of this view of equal opportunity.

Yet the depiction of equal employment opportunity suggested by the *Griggs* decision broadens awareness of the barriers to equal opportunity. *Griggs* states: "the methods and procedures which employment institutions use to determine ability and industry must be valid." If their validity cannot be demonstrated, then those screened out by such methods and procedures have been discriminated against: "If an employment practice which operated to exclude Negroes cannot be shown to be related to job performance, the practice is prohibited."[117] The Supreme Court here states quite explicitly that equality in employment extends beyond ". . . overt discrimination . . ." and also includes ". . . practices that are fair in form, but discriminatory in operation."[118] The Court elaborated on this point: "any test used must measure the person for the job and not the person in the abstract."[119] This implies that inappropriate tests contrive an abstract model of a qualified applicant. Likewise, general ability tests assume that anyone who is qualified for any job must have a certain ability, e.g., some degree of mechanical proficiency. However, even if a test measures this aptitude accurately, it may be irrelevant to a particular job(s). The Court, therefore, has invited questions regarding the abstract methods of tests for use in discerning merit.

The *Griggs* opinion provided a defense of affirmative action practice guidelines that had been explicated by the EEOC in 1966, 1967, and 1970. In its annual report of 1967, EEOC found that verbal aptitude tests were often used in jobs that required few verbal skills. EEOC also found that this selection method had negative effects on minorities.[120] In 1970, EEOC stipulated that employment tests be validated by "data demonstrating that the test is predictive of or significantly correlated with important elements of work behavior which comprise or are relevant to the job or jobs for which candidates are being evaluated."[121] These guidelines intended to discourage inadvertent present discrimination as identified in *Griggs'* broad critique of traditional conceptions of equal opportunity. The *Griggs* opinion defends the affirmative action goal of non-discrimination, but the case did not receive the national attention as did *Bakke* and recent events in Michigan.

Michael Lewis argues that Americans have traditionally believed that the "individual is central" and accordingly, that the individual alone is responsible for his or her success or failure.[122] Robert Bellah and his co-authors underscore this argument by declaring that individualism is our "deepest identity."[123] Bellah believes the origin of Americans' individualism is John Locke's notion that the individual, existing prior to society and government, creates the two out of a desire to pursue self-interest in an appropriate setting.[124] What Bellah could have added here is that the Lockean depiction of the individual presupposes one who is naturally fully equipped to handle all that comes his way because he is endowed with reason. According to Locke, it is ". . . the industrious and rational . . . not . . . the quarrelsome and contentious" who prosper.[125] Similarly, the American love of "making our own decisions" is engaged when, according to Bellah's depiction, we harness that rationality and industry to achieve a high test score and/or academic degree, which many of us believe are the keys to achieving our personal desires.

These depictions of American individualism suggest a free will which, according to Nicholas Capaldi, ". . . is something more fundamental than the environment . . ."[126] Capaldi believes that for victims of past discrimination, ". . . what is most important is to take personal responsibility."[127] Therefore, one can assume that Capaldi believes that "personal responsibility" can overcome present discrimination. The depictions of American individualism explicated by Lewis, Bellah, and Capaldi suggest that many Americans, despite oppressive environments, believe that the economic fate of the individual is in his or her own hands. Such a perspective would not perceive as crucial such factors as institutional, structural, or covert phenomena. It would tend, rather, to deem institutional racism or class disadvantage only as temporary barriers to individual achievement for an individual who is consistently industrious and rational. The intellectual result is an exalted view of individual self-determination; Americans do not believe that institutions, economic trends, or personal economic power influence the attainment of goals. There is, according to this view, basically one type of person in America: the 'free' individual. This autonomous individual is viewed as a nearly eternal source of power because all forms of oppression are, however externally-rooted, highly surmountable. According to this view, the only impediments to individual achievement are the individual's identification of himself as a victim of oppression,[128] and overt present discrimination. One political result of this prominent American ideology is opposition to affirmative action, which appears to reward those who fail to exert sufficient individual effort.

Political and academic reactions to *Griggs* serve to confirm Louis Hartz's argument concerning American political culture. The "irrational" attachment to Lockean concepts[129] that Hartz saw in Americans engendered a belief that *Griggs* endangered individual liberty. Herman Belz wrote: "*Griggs* shifted civil rights policy to a . . . equality-of-result rationale that made the social consequences of employment practices, rather than their purposes, intent, or motivation, the decisive consideration in determining their lawfulness."[130] Belz links *Griggs* to "the war against testing," and treats the purposes and intent of employment tests as legitimate, if they are not used to discriminate. In so doing he upholds the liberal concept of employer freedom, but ignores the Court's point that employees who had not taken the employment tests or did not have the requisite degree still performed their jobs satisfactorily. Belz' equation of *Griggs* with equality of result misses the point that the decision had nothing to do with proportional representation, but rather, with fairness in selection methods. This distinction is truly liberal, by promoting fairness and relevance of selection criteria, *Griggs* enhances the opportunities for economic mobility and facilitates individual liberty.

Political elite reactions to *Griggs* have also reflected a distortion of "business necessity." James C. Sharf, of the Reagan Administration's Office of Personnel Management, equates *Griggs* with ". . . the trashing of objective employment standards . . . [which] may well have contributed to this nation's productivity decline."[131] As with Belz, Sharf ignored the Court's showing that the tests in question and the degree requirements had no relationship to job performance. The major thrusts of the *Griggs* decision have never entered the realm of public discussion, and rarely have publicly visible political defenders of affirmative action endorsed the business necessity principle for credentials and tests.

SUMMARY

This chapter has shown that both opposition to affirmative action and defenses of the policy have not rationally analyzed traditional conceptions of merit. Chapter two will show that such conceptions, if institutionalized, would discriminate against many qualified African-Americans, and significantly impair the social goals of diversity and fairness.

NOTES

1. Mary Frances Berry, *Black Resistance, White Law* (New York: Meredith Corporation, 1971), p.180

2. 387 U.S. 483 (1954).

3. Berry, *Black Resistance, White Law*.

4. Albert G. Mosley and Nicholas Capaldi, *Affirmative Action* (New York: Rowman and Littlefield, Inc., 1996), p.2.

5. Paul Burstein, *Discrimination, Jobs, and Politics* (Chicago: University of Chicago Press, 1985), p. 95.

6. Carl M. Brauer, *John F. Kennedy and the Second Reconstruction* (Chicago: University of Chicago Press, 1985), p.95.

7. Ibid., pp.58–59.

8. Ibid., chapter two.

9. Ibid., p.79.

10. 3 C.F.R. 1959–1963 Comp., p.450.

11. Ibid., p.448.

12. Carl M. Brauer, John F. Kennedy and the Second Reconstruction (New York: Columbia Press, 1977), p.83.

13. Ibid., pp.147–151 and 214–216.

14. U.S., Civil Service Commission, *Study of Minority Group Employment in the Federal Government*: 1965 (Washington, D.C.: Government Printing Office, 1965).

15. Brauer, *Second Reconstruction*, p. 285.

16. *Public Papers of the Presidents*: Lyndon Johnson, 1965 (Washington, D.C.: Government Printing Office, 1965), 2:636.

17. C.F.R. 1964–1965 Comp., pp.339–48.

18. James C. Harvey, *Black Civil Rights During the Johnson Administration* (Jackson: University And College Press of Mississippi, 1973), p.123.

19. Ibid., pp.118–122.

20. Ibid., pp. 127–128.

21. Ibid., p.147.

22. Richard P. Nathan, *Jobs and Civil Rights* (Washington, D.C.: U.S. Government Printing Office, 1969), pp.39–40

23. Hugh Davis Graham, *The Civil Rights Era: Origins and Development of National Policy*, 1960–1972 New York: Oxford University Press, 1990), pp. 149–150. Illinois FEPC Charge No. 63x-127, quoted in Graham, *The Civil Rights Era*, p.149.

24. *The Civil Rights Act of 1964* (Washington, D.C.: BNA Incorporated, 1964), p.120.

25. Graham, *The Civil Rights Era*, pp.139–140.

26. The *Civil Rights Act of 1964*, pp.120–121.

27. 110 *Congressional Record*, Pt. 5, 30 March 1964, p.6549.

28. *The Civil Rights Act of 1964*, p.329.

29. Hugh Davis Graham, *The Civil Rights Era: Origins and Development of National Policy*, 1960–1972 (New York: Oxford University Press, 1990), p.327.

30. Title 41, C.F.R., 60–2.11.

31. Ibid., 60-2.2.

32. Graham, Civil Rights Era, p.339.

33. Congress, Senate, Subcommittee on Separation of Powers of the Senate Committee on the Judiciary, *Hearings: The Philadelphia Plan and S. 931*, 91st Congress, 1st Session, 27–28 October 1969.

34. See Fred L. Pincus, *Reverse Discrimination: Dismantling the Myth* (Boulder: Lynne Rienner Publishers, 2003), chap.4.

35. 401 U.S. 424 (1971) at 431.

36. Ibid.

37. Nathan Glazer, *Ethnic Dilemmas 1964–1982* (Cambridge, Massachusetts: Harvard University Press, 1983); Herman Belz, *Equality Transformed* (New Brunswick, New Jersey: Transaction Publishers, 1991); Robert R. Detlefsen, *Civil Rights Under Reagan* (San Francisco: ICS Press, 1991).

38. The Civil Rights Act of 1964, p.303.

39. 3 C.F.R. 1959–1963 Comp., p.448.

40. Ibid., p.449.

41. Carl M. Brauer, *John F. Kennedy and the Second Reconstruction* (New York: Columbia University Press, 1977), p.5.

42. Ibid., p.276.

43. See Glazer, *Ethnic Dilemmas 1964–1972* (Cambridge, Mass.: Harvard University Press, 1983), chap.9; Graham, *The Civil Rights Era*; Belz, *Equality Transformed* (New Brunswick, N.J.: Transaction Publishers, 1991); Detfelsen, *Civil Rights Under Reagan* (San Francisco: ICS Press, 1991).

44. Brauer, *John F. Kennedy and the Second Reconstruction*, p. 277.

45. John David Skrentny, *The Ironies of Affirmative Action* (Chicago: The University of Chicago Press, 1996), p. 27.

46. Ibid.

47. Graham, *The Civil Rights Era*, pp.323.

48. Ibid., p.327.

49. Ibid., p.337.

50. Ibid., pp.327,337.

51. Hugh Davis Graham, "The Origins of Affirmative Action: Civil Rights and the Regulatory State", in *The ANNALS of the American Academy of Political and Social Science*, Volume 523, eds. Harold Orlans and June O'Neil (Newbury Park: SAGE Publications, Inc., 1992), pp.56–57.

52. See Michael Walzer, Spheres of Justice (New York: Basic Books, 1983), pp.142–143.

53. Alexandra K. Wigdor and Wendell R. Garner, eds., *Ability Testing: Uses, Consequences, and Controversies*, Part I and II (Washington D.C.: National Academy Press, 1982), Part I, p.72.

54. Skrentny, *Ironies*, p.27.

55. Graham, *The Civil Rights Era*, p.337.

56. Ibid., p.323.

57. *Congress and the Nation*, Volume III (Washington, D.C.: Congressional Quarterly, 1973), p.498.

58. Graham, *The Civil Rights Era*, pp.149–150.

59. 401 U.S. 424 (1971) at 431.

60. Ibid., at 430.

61. Ibid., at 431–432.

62. 401 U.S. 424 (1971) at 431.

63. Belz, *Equality Transformed*, pp.146–148; Bernard Schwartz, *Behind Bakke: Affirmative Action and the Supreme Court* (New York: New York University Press, 1988), p.1.

64. See Graham, *The Civil Rights Era*.

65. Nathan Glazer, *Affirmative Discrimination* (Cambridge, MA: Harvard University Press: 1975); Sydney Hook, "Discrimination, Color Blindness, and the Quota System", *Measure*, 14, (October, 1971); Barry R. Gross, ed., *Reverse Discrimination* (Buffalo: Prometheus Books, 1977).

66. Belz, *Equality Transformed*, p.148.

67. See Schwartz, especially chaps. 1,2,13.

68. 438 U.S. 265 (1978) at 265.

69. Ibid., at 320.

70. Ibid., at 307–310.

71. Ibid., at 320.

72. Ibid., at 313.

73. Ibid., at 314, 311.

74. Ibid., at 318.

75. Ibid.

76. See Michael Lewis, *The Culture of Inequality* (Amherst: University of Massachusetts Press, 1978), especially chaps. 1, 4, 5 and Herbert McCloskey and John Zaller, *American Ethos* (Cambridge, Mass: Harvard University Press, 1984) especially chaps. 3,4,7.

77. 438 U.S. 265 (1978) at 313.

78. William Raspberry, "Why Civil Rights Isn't Selling", *Washington Post*, 13 March 1991.

79. Thomas Byrne Edsall and Mary D. Edsall, *Chain Reaction* (New York: W.W. Norton and Company, 1992), p.255.

80. Ibid., p.191.

81. John Edwards, When Race Counts: *The Morality of Racial Preference in Britain and America* (London and New York; Routledge, 1995) p.122.

82. 490 U.S. 642 (1989) at 657.

83. Ibid., at 659.

84. Ibid., at 650.

85. Ibid., at 652.

86. Ibid., at 659.

87. 401 U.S. 424 (1971) at 431.

88. 490 U.S. 642 (1989) at 661.

89. *U.S. Code, Congressional and Administrative News*, 102nd Congress—1st Session 1991, Volume 2 (St. Paul Minnesota: West Publishing Company, 1991), p.568.

90. *Civil Rights Act of 1991* (Chicago: Commerce Clearing House, Inc.: 1991), p.73.

91. Ibid., p.75.

92. 401 U.S. 424 (1971) at 432.

93. Civil Rights Act of 1991, p.75.

94. 440 U.S. 568 (1979).

95. 490 U.S. 642 (1989) at 659.

96. *Civil Rights Act of 1991*, p.75.

97. *U.S. Code, Congressional and Administrative News*, 102nd Congress—1st Session 1991, Volume 2 (St. Paul Minnesota: West Publishing Company, 1991), p.568.

98. 440 U.S. 568 (1979).

99. These observations come from my work with methadone patients in 1985–1986.

100. George R. LaNoue, "Split Visions: Minority Business Set-Asides", in *The Annals of the American Academy of Political and Social Science*, Volume 523, p.115; *Philadelphia Inquirer*, February 19, 1997, A1.

101. Terry Eastland, *Ending Affirmative Action* (New York: Basic Books, 1996), p.128.

102. Philadelphia Inquirer, November 28, 2001, A3.

103. Philadelphia Inquirer, November 18, 2001, A10.

104. *New York Times*, March 7, 1998, A9.

105. *Philadelphia Inquirer*, November 28, 1996, A20.

106. *Philadelphia Inquirer*, February 23, 2000, A3.

107. *Philadelphia Inquirer*, December 21, 1996, A6.

108. *Philadelphia Inquirer*, April 9, 1997, A2.

109. *Philadelphia Inquirer,* November 20, 1997, A1.

110. *Philadelphia Inquirer*, June 15, 1997, A1, A8.

111. *Philadelphia Inquirer*, April 9, 1997, A2.

112. *Philadelphia Inquirer*, July 20, 1995, A1.

113. *Philadelphia Inquirer*, August 29, 2003, A2.

114. *Philadelphia Inquirer*, August 29, 2003, A2 and *Philadelphia Inquirer*, June 24, 2003, A1, A8, A9.

115. *Philadelphia Inquirer*, March 12, 2004, A2 and *Philadelphia Inquirer,* June 14, 2004, A4.

116. Skrentny, *Ironies*, p.27.

117. 401 U.S. 424 (1971) at 431.

118. Ibid.

119. Ibid., at 436.

120. Harvey, *Black Civil Rights During the Johnson Administration* (Jackson: University and College Press of Mississippi, 1973), pp.133–134.

121. 401 U.S. 424 (1971) at 433.

122. Lewis, *The Culture of Inequality* (Amherst: University of Massachusetts Press, 1978), chap. 1.

123. Robert N. Bellah, et. al., *Habits of the Heart: Individualism and Commitment in American Life* (New York: Harper and Row, 1985), p.142.

124. Ibid., p.143.

125. John Locke, *The Second Treatise of Government* (New York; MacMillian Publishing Company: 1952), chap. II.

126. Mosley and Capaldi, *Affirmative Action* (Lanham, Maryland: Rowman and Littlefield Publishers, Inc., 1996), p.100.

127. Ibid.

128. Ibid., pp.65-105.

129. Louis Hartz, *The Liberal Tradition in America* (Harcourt Brace Jovanovich, Inc.: 1955) in *The American Polity Reader*, Second Edition, eds. Ann G. Serow, W. Wayne Shannon, Everett C. Ladd (New York: W.W. Norton and Company: 1993), pp.14-20.

130. Belz, *Equality Transformed*, p.51.

131. James C. Sharf, "Litigating Personnel Measurment Policy", Journal of Vocational Behavior, December 1988, quoted in Edsall and Edsall, *Chain Reaction*, p.253.

Chapter Two

Affirmative Action:
Necessity and Success

The previous chapter suggested that affirmative action programs are necessary since a return to solely traditional concepts of merit in the higher education and employment selection process would bar many African-Americans from higher education opportunities and jobs. Such practices, traditional concepts of merit, constitute a form of present discrimination, but affirmative action is needed to thwart this, and to maintain a steady progress toward society's diversity goals by allowing qualified African-Americans to be identified and given opportunities. This chapter provides evidence of the negative effects on African-Americans if institutions rely solely on traditional selection criteria, and also shows how affirmative action successes suggest that a broader range of relevant criteria, which affirmative action programs and some institutions use, is viable and necessary for identifying qualified African-Americans and accomplishing the social benefits of diversity.

TRADITIONAL METHODS OF SELECTION

Broadly speaking, formal traditional criteria for college admission includes tests, grades, interviews, references, essays, geographical status, extra-curricular activities, family legacy, and informal things such as family status, money contributed to the institution, and contacts. Traditional selection criteria for jobs include tests, for some jobs, grades, to a lesser degree than for higher education,[1] job experience, interviews, references and more informal practices like patronage and contacts. Affirmative action programs which add race, gender and physical disability to the list of qualifications broaden the range of criteria. Race is not a traditional criterion unless one considers that being white was and is still in some institutions[2] a criterion for employment and promotion. Non-traditional criteria for higher education includes ESL (English as a second language) applicants, being the first in a family to attend college, overcoming environmental difficulties, and graduating in the top 10% of a high school class.[3] Being black, Hispanic, female, or handicapped are non traditional qualifications. Affirmative action practices, at times, involve lowering the bar on some traditional criteria and focusing on other traditional and non-traditional ones.

THE NARROW FOCUS OF
AFFIRMATIVE ACTION OPPONENTS

The "list" of formal, traditional selection criteria for both higher education and jobs constitute, excepting the absence of race and gender and lowering the bar on test scores and grades, a broad range of qualifications *if many* are used for selecting candidates. The problem for diversity and fairness occurs when institutions use just a few qualifications in the selection process, or a few are controlling such as tests and, or grades. This approach to ensuring fairness in the selection process was noted by the Supreme Court in *Griggs* ". . . tests are useful servants, but . . . they are not to become masters of reality."[4] The claim that affirmative action is unfair because it chooses unqualified or less qualified racial minorities and women over more qualified whites and men implies that tests and grades be controlling factors. Much of the affirmative action controversy is generated by reified views of tests and grades. These claims often arise when opponents of affirmative action perceive that a white law school applicant with a higher LSAT (Law School Admissions Test) score and, or higher grades than an African-American applicant from the same pool, is more qualified for admission. Opponents overlook or ignore the broad mix of criteria that the law school may have used to select the African-American applicant.

A number of high profile affirmative action cases demonstrate that affirmative action opponents often view tests and grades as controlling selection criteria. The 2003 cases of *Grutter v. Bollinger* and *Gratz v. Bollinger*, which looked at affirmative action policies at the University of Michigan, began when the plaintiff in the former case sued because she was rejected by the law school despite having a 3.8 grade point average and ranking in the 86th percentile on the LSAT.[5] Grutter claimed that she was denied admission to the law school because its affirmative action policy favored admitting less-qualified[6] minorities. The law school's admission process considers race as one of many factors[7] as it tries to ensure that minorities make up a critical mass of 10 percent to 12 percent of each incoming class.[8] The University of Michigan's undergraduate admissions process, scrutinized in *Gratz*, also considered race as one of many factors, but was challenged on the same grounds as *Grutter*.[9]

In 2001, a case heard by a federal appeals court panel involved the affirmative action admissions program at the University of Georgia, which looked at 12 factors for students who were not automatically admitted on the basis of their grades and standardized tests, but whose grades and scores were close to school cut-offs. A high score on the 12 factors which constituted the Total Student Index (TSI) gained admission for such students.[10] Since the TSI was used for applicants who were close to the University of Georgia's test scores and grade point average (GPA) requirements, opponents of the admissions process clearly believe that tests and grades hold inordinate weight and thereby dismiss using a broad range approach in the college admissions selection process. To critics of affirmative action, test and GPA cut-offs establish a line of demarcation between the less and more qualified which—to them—stands on unshakable intellectual ground.

The case of *Hopwood v. Texas*, heard by the United States Court of Appeals for the Fifth Circuit, further illustrates the reified view of test scores and GPA taken by affirmative action opponents. The white plaintiffs in *Hopwood* argued that their GPA and LSAT scores would have gained them admission to the University of Texas Law School if they had been of a different race.[11] However, the Law School also considered state residency and the strength of the undergraduate colleges the applicants attended, as well as trying to achieve an African-American enrollment of 5% and a Mexican-American enrollment of 10%.[12] The plaintiffs assumed that GPA and LSAT scores are flawless predictors of descending and ascending degrees of qualification. The median GPA for the in-coming class of non-minorities at the law school was 3.56 and the median LSAT was 164, while the median GPA for African-Americans was 3.30 and the median LSAT was 158.[13] It is hard to say that the relatively slight differences of the two groups of applicants can determine the whites to be more qualified to succeed in the Law School. Such a claim assigns to the LSAT and to the GPA an ability to objectively rank order all applicants, and—when implied in the arguments of affirmative action critics—this claim obscures the social import of having a significant percent of qualified African-Americans in the Law School.

THE PROBLEMS OF A REIFIED VIEW OF MERIT

Education

A number of studies support the view that the centerpiece of affirmative action opposition—higher test scores and GPA equals more qualified higher

education applicants—is flawed, and if instituted would have unjust outcomes for African-Americans. Theodore Cross calculates the impact that undergraduate and professional school admissions policies, if test scores were
controlling criteria, would have on African-Americans. According to Cross,
the percentage of blacks enrolled in the 25 top-rated universities in the fall of
1994 was 6.2 percent, but this figure would drop to 1.5 percent if the mean
SAT score were used as an admissions cut-off score.[14] These decreases in
black enrollment would have reduced the 3000 blacks in the top 25 universities in 1994 to 700. African-American enrollment at the nation's top 20 law
schools and in medical schools would have dropped in 1994 from 500 to 100
and 4,000 to 1,000, respectively, if LSAT and MCAT(Medical School Admissions Test) determined admissions. However, all African-American college applicants, not just those applying to the most selective schools would be
affected by giving test scores such inordinate weight. Considering that, nationally, blacks, on average, score 200 points below the white mean on the
SAT, 19 percent lower on the LSAT, and 2.2 points(on a 15 point scale) lower
than whites on the MCAT,[15] admissions policies informed by a strict ranking
of applicants based on scores on these tests would result in very few blacks
admitted to schools whose applicant pools were predominantly white.

Arguments that the SAT, MCAT, and LSAT often correctly identify who is
and is not qualified for undergraduate law and medical school are disputed by
various studies. James Crouse and Dale Trusheim found that when the SAT is
added to high school rank the predicted college grades of African-American
college applicants drops and lowers black admissions by 16.9 percent. The
critical finding of this study, however, is that the SAT would decrease the
number of blacks who would earn a bachelors degree by 9.5 percent by not
admitting them due to a false negative prediction.[16] The effect on blacks in
real numbers is close to 224 qualified blacks out of every 1,000 black applicants being rejected if high school rank and the SAT are combined to predict
college grades and thereby determine admission or non-admission.[17]

A 1997 study by William G. Bowen and Derek Bok of selective colleges
and universities reports that race-neutral admissions policies, requiring blacks
to have the same mean MCAT, LSAT and GPA as whites, would decrease
black enrollment in elite medical and law schools to 1 percent of the student
body.[18] Their more compelling finding, however, shows that, of the black students who entered a selective school in 1976, 9 percent went on to earn a
medical degree, slightly better than the 7 percent figure for whites. This reveals that, given the opportunity, African-Americans will pursue and attain
their professional goals, but many would have their chance denied if strict
rank-ordering based on the MCAT is employed.[19] When one considers that
the average mean MCAT for accepted African-Americans is 7.4, but the av-

erage for rejected whites is 8.0, the adverse and unjust results of race-neutral selection becomes clear.[20]

The unfair outcomes of using MCAT scores alone, or with GPA as controlling selection criteria are further illustrated by a 1997 study of the University of California at Davis Medical School's affirmative action program, conducted over twenty years, which finds that ninety-four percent of affirmative action students graduated, compared to ninety-seven percent of students admitted through traditional standards. The mean undergraduate GPA of the affirmative action admittees is 3.06 compared to 3.5 for students admitted through normal standards. The non-traditional admittees also had MCAT scores below standard criteria. If Davis had used traditional grade and MCAT cut-offs, ninety-six percent of its minority medical students would have been rejected. But the fact remains that most of them have graduated.[21] Since law schools also frequently admit minorities with lower test scores and grades than whites,[22] the twenty-five percent increase in black doctors and lawyers, from 1977 to 1987,[23] would not have occurred if traditional criteria had determined admissions. The Davis Medical School's affirmative action program considers race, fluency in multiple languages, economic disadvantage, leadership qualities, unique life experiences, and physical disability, *in addition to* grades and test scores. Davis' program debunks perceptions that tests and grades should be controlling admissions factors; that they are best at determining academic qualifications.

The use of LSAT scores as cut-offs would reject many qualified black law school candidates. Linda Wightman found that for 30 of the most selective law schools, the average LSAT score was 24 percent higher for whites than for blacks,[24] but if race-neutral criteria, LSAT and GPA, were the sole determiners of admission, black enrollment in these law schools would decrease from 6.5 percent to 1 percent.[25] However, 91 percent of blacks at the 30 most selective law schools graduated.[26] 78 percent of blacks from 163 ABA–approved law schools graduated,[27] despite many having been admitted without the normal LSAT and GPA requirements.[28]

Similar to test scores, GPA or class rank produce unjust results for African-Americans when used to establish cut-offs and as controlling admissions criteria for higher education. As previously discussed, the mean GPA for affirmative action beneficiaries in the Davis study was 3.06 compared to 3.5 for students admitted using normal Davis Medical School standards, but 94 percent of the affirmative action admittees graduated.[29] Crouse and Trusheim found that, if class rank or GPA is used to predict if African-American applicants will attain a bachelor's degree and schools reject those who, according to this criterion would not, nearly 130 qualified blacks out of every 1,000 black applicants will be denied admission to college.[30] Bowen and Bok's study also calls into question the belief that class rank is reliable enough to be a sole predictor of academic success. Their study shows that 68 percent of blacks who graduated in the middle third of their class at 28 selective colleges and universities earned advanced degrees, and 50 percent of those earned professional or doctoral degrees. At these schools, 49 percent of blacks in the bottom third earned advanced degrees, with 34 percent earning professional or doctoral degrees.[31] Considering that many blacks from the Bowen and Bok study earned their advanced degrees despite having lower undergraduate and high school grades than most other students,[32] the view that affirmative action provides a fairer equal opportunity than does that based on ranking according to GPA and, or tests is supported.

Employment

As discussed in the previous chapter, the Supreme Court in *Griggs* argued that job qualifications which eliminate significant percentages of blacks had to be shown to be job-related or a business necessity.[33] These concepts will be addressed as guidelines for fair selection criteria in chapter four. For present purposes, *Griggs* is relevant because it presents evidence that tests used for selecting or eliminating job applicants screened out large numbers of blacks, while blacks who did not take the tests continued to perform well in jobs at Duke Power after the tests were used.[34] The previous section demonstrated that if tests and GPA are the sole selection criteria, the number of qualified blacks admitted to colleges will decrease. This section will provide evidence that tests cannot be controlling criteria for job selection if fairness to African-Americans is to be maintained, and then will show that affirmative action beneficiaries do not perform worse than others in jobs, and therefore, cannot be labeled less qualified or unqualified.

John Hartigan and Alexandra Wigdor point out that blacks perform worse, on average, than whites on employment tests.[35] However, Hartigan and Wigdor reporting for the National Research Council (NRC) found that the General Aptitude Test Battery (GATB) screened out one-half of the successful black carpenters who participated in its study of the GATB. If these carpenters had been rank-ordered for jobs, according to their GATB scores, none of them would have been referred for employment.[36] The NRC study also reported that the lower average scores of blacks, as compared to whites, on the Armed Services Vocational Aptitude Battery (ASVAB) may not be indicative of ability deficits. Blacks, on average, scored much closer to whites on hands-on measures of job performance than they did on the paper and pencil sections of the test battery.[37] The ASVAB study suggests that if African-Americans do fairly well on those parts of tests which are more related to actual job performance, they may be qualified. A number of studies which looked at the performance of affirmative action beneficiaries support the implication of the NRC studies, and of *Griggs*.

PERFORMANCE OF AFFIRMATIVE ACTION BENEFICIARIES

If it can be shown that those hired through affirmative action are not less qualified than those hired through traditional means, then the reverse discrimination claim, as discussed in the previous chapter, is without merit. Harry Holzer and David Neumark surveyed 800 places of employment in the Atlanta, Detroit, Boston and Los Angeles metropolitan areas. Performance ratings, education, promotion, wages and other qualifications of over 3,000 workers hired into entry-level jobs were analyzed. Two important findings emerged from the study. Minorities hired through affirmative action tended to have relatively lower educational or skill requirements than non-beneficiaries of affirmative action,[38] but did not perform worse than those hired through traditional selection approaches.[39] This study suggests that what may appear to be a less qualified job candidate, on paper, may not be, and that employers who use affirmative action do not consider some traditional indicators of who should not be selected to be controlling criteria.

A survey of 100 of the largest businesses in Chicago from 1975 to 1987, conducted by Major G. Coleman, found no statistical significance between cost and efficiency and percentage of minorities in a business.[40] A similar appraisal of affirmative action hires was reported by Jonathan Leonard. Leonard studied 68,000 businesses for the years 1974–1980, and found that while affirmative action increased relative black employment, it did not adversely affect these firms' productivity.[41] Leonard based this finding on the fact that firms that hired more minorities, through affirmative action, showed nearly identical growth rates with firms that hired fewer minorities.[42] A national study by Nicholas P. Lovrich, Brent S. Steel, and David Hood, based on a study of more than 250 United States municipal police departments, also found that affirmative action exacted marginal negative costs for the public in terms of efficient law enforcement.[43] Lovrich, et. al, compared police departments which did more affirmative action hiring with those doing less. They reported that operational costs, crime rates, apprehension of criminals, and allocation of expenditures for non-essential services were not seriously affected in departments where affirmative action efforts were high.[44] Both of these studies suggest that, contrary to the perceptions of affirmative action critics and public opinion, race-conscious policies do not hire many unqualified minorities. The *Griggs* case is important because it implicitly questions the

assumption of affirmative action critics who argue that tests and a higher educational level accurately identify ranks among job candidates. The NRC
studies can be allied with *Griggs* to further question the opponents of affirmative action who assign air-tight predictive power to tests and educational
attainment. However, *Griggs* and the NRC studies question traditional ideas
of merit and the various studies which suggest that affirmative action beneficiaries are not less qualified than other hires suggests that a broad range of
qualifications must be used by employers. Affirmative action is necessary
since many qualified African-Americans would be eliminated from consideration for employment if tests and education level were given inordinate
weight in the selection process. It can also be ascertained from the previously
discussed studies that employers who use affirmative action implicitly acknowledge the limitations of a narrow meaning of merit since employment
establishments are not hurt by affirmative action.

Public Contracts

The previous chapter discussed the origins of the use of affirmative action for
public contracts. To summarize, past racial discrimination had made businesses owned by African-Americans less likely to get government contracts.
The effects of racial discrimination, economic and social marginalization,
rendered black-owned businesses less qualified due to deficient amounts of
capital, inadequate knowledge of bidding procedure and difficulty meeting
bonding requirements.[45] These barriers, coupled with the disfavoring of minority businesses by government offices, gave rise to minority business set-
asides and procurement officials assigned to help such businesses receive
public contracts.[46] This section will show that, though a disproportionate percentage of government contracts continue to go to non-minority businesses,
many black-owned businesses using government programs have done well.

Racial disparity in contract awards continues to be evident. The Clinton administration found that, as of 1997, minority-owned businesses received only
5.5 percent of federal contracting funds.[47] Equally compelling is an Associated Press analysis of the Small Business Administration's (SBA) program,
which directs federal contracts to minority-owned companies. The analysis
found that only 22 percent of the program's dollars went to businesses in minority areas, despite SBA's claim that its program attempts to boost job opportunities in minority regions.[48] Since 78 percent of SBA's dollars go to
businesses in non-minority regions, minority access to jobs created by SBA
is limited.

Beyond the continuing disparities in contract awards, one of the central
purposes of affirmative action is to familiarize black businesses with the re-

quirements necessary for competitiveness, regarding both the business market and getting contracts. George R. LaNoue, studying minority business enterprises (MBEs), has found that black-owned businesses grew by more than 115,000 from 1982 to 1987. LaNoue finds that "[MBEs] . . . provided training, capital, and networks for new [MBEs] and have obliged older businesses to share opportunities with them."[49] Farrell Bloch corroborates the benefits of minority-owned businesses by pointing out that they create jobs, increase minority suppliers, and thereby "enrich job-seeking networks within the community."[50]

Further evidence of the success of affirmative action in contracting is provided by Timothy Bates. Previous studies had shown that black mayors placed a high priority on helping black-owned businesses.[51] Bates studied 28 large metropolitan areas and found that 72.9 percent of black-owned businesses in the 10 cities with African-American mayors were still operating at the time of the study and 66.9 percent of like businesses were operating in metropolitan areas with non-black mayors.[52] Bates also showed that while greater success for black-owned businesses occurred in non-minority areas, these firms still aided inner-city residents and economies; 78.9 percent of such businesses had 75 percent or more black employees, whereas 62 percent of white firms had no black employees.[53] Even when white firms are located in minority communities, 32.9 percent of these businesses have no black employees and only 37.6 percent of such businesses have 50 percent or more African-American workers, but 93.1 percent of businesses owned by African-Americans operating in minority communities had minority employment of 75 percent or more.[54]

The continuing disproportionate share of federal contracts going to African-American entrepreneurs suggests that, absent affirmative action efforts, minority awards would be even fewer. However, LaNoue and Bates show that government programs help minority businesses get into the loop and become more competitive in the procurement process, and both have also shown that affirmative action can claim many successes. Considering the latter point, those who oppose affirmative action for public contracts cannot legitimately claim that unqualified, or less qualified, entrepreneurs are—across the board—given public funds that end up as a waste of money, nor can opponents claim that such programs are discriminatory.

MERIT

The defense of affirmative action argued in this chapter debunks traditional conceptions of merit. Such concepts of merit are rooted in American political culture. According to John Skrentny, Americans traditionally believed that government should "[g]ive people the freedom to pursue their ends and make contracts, and justice will result." This same tradition sanctions the belief that "[t]he land of opportunity was . . . meritocratic: one deserved all that one could attain by talent and industry."[55] According to this view, equal opportunity is contingent upon a vaguely defined contractual freedom; as long as all possess this "freedom," all are unfettered in their pursuit of goals. The achievement of individual goals depends upon individual talent, initiative, and hard work. The central thrust in the *Griggs* decision, however, is that selection methods must accurately discern ability and non-ability for the specific job(s) for which they are employed. The traditional view of equal opportunity collides with *Griggs* on the concept of merit. While Griggs does not question the notion that ability and hard work are important employee attributes, it also notes that talent and industry cannot be discerned by ". . . general testing devices . . ."[56] Accordingly, those who are denied college admission, employment or promotion through, for example, lower test scores and GPA have not been accorded the opportunity to demonstrate their talent and industry. The traditional notion of equal opportunity implies that talent and industry will reveal themselves through objective tests, but the evidence presented in this chapter suggests that tests and GPA must not be accorded inordinate influence; they cannot be controlling criteria.

RANK ORDERING

Traditional merit concepts suggest that selection officers or committees can objectively rank order a pool of job or higher education applicants. Job and higher education selectees must be good risks. Some jobs require specific skills, and academic ability or its potential must be evident in those admitted to colleges. But employers and admissions officers can discriminate when they give inordinate weight to some criteria, as when they say, "This job cannot be performed successfully, or academic success will not occur unless candidates have a certain GPA", or "The applicant with the higher test score is definitely more qualified." But why, for example, is an entry-level psychotherapist who has higher grades than others considered more qualified? Someone who seeks an entry-level psychotherapist position and who has performed well in a related internship may be qualified. Of the candidates who fulfill this necessary criteria, some will be better writers; others may have skill at presenting seminars; still another may have personality traits which foster a positive work environment; or others may help serve minority clients. Still others will have higher GPAs, or some may display a strong desire to grow professionally as a therapist. The point is that all of these candidates fulfill the necessary criteria, and each also has other relevant abilities. It is not likely that anyone has all of these related but non-essential skills. Higher grades may suggest good self-discipline, but such applicants are not necessarily more qualified than those with excellent writing skills, or those who display a strong liking for their jobs and co-workers. High grades are not irrelevant in this case, but they are also not essential. Of greatest significance here is that all of these entry-level candidates are qualified, but it is difficult, if not impossible, to determine which one is the "best" qualified.[57]

The *Griggs* opinion argued that only relevant selection criteria are fair, but did not critique the objectivity of a strict rank-ordering of qualified applicants. Critiquing this practice is crucial if popular support for affirmative action is to increase. Americans must be shown that a law school applicant with a 3.4 GPA and 41 on the LSAT is not necessarily more qualified to do well in law school than another who has a 3.1 GPA and a 38 LSAT score. Opposition to affirmative action revolves around the belief that the former applicant is objectively more qualified. However, as Michael Walzer points out, it is difficult to rank-order candidates who possess the relevant qualifications.[58] A line can be drawn between the qualified and the unqualified, but among those who are above the line, assigning degrees of ability gets murkier. A prospective teacher at any educational level must be fairly articulate; but of those who are, determining which one is the most well-spoken is a more subjective process than discerning who can, and who cannot, communicate effectively. Effective teachers must be articulate, organize their presentations clearly, and possess good interpersonal skills. Among those who satisfy these necessary criteria, it is difficult to determine, in advance, that one teacher is more qualified than the others.

TRADITIONAL CONCEPTIONS OF MERIT AS DISCRIMINATION

The belief that a college or job applicant with a higher test score and, or GPA is more qualified than one with a lower test score or GPA can unduly influence selection decisions. If traditional notions of the infallibility of tests to distinguish the qualified from the unqualified, and the belief that tests can objectively determine ordinal rankings of the qualified inform selection, then a form of discrimination will occur. The various studies discussed in this chapter indicate that large numbers of qualified African-Americans would be denied admission to colleges and would be less likely to be hired if reified concepts of merit and rank-ordering are given inordinate power in selection processes. Affirmative action is necessary because it implicitly recognizes that a strict traditional conception of merit will discriminate against many African-Americans and would dramatically weaken efforts to diversify American institutions.

AN ALTERNATIVE APPROACH TO SELECTION

As has been shown, using traditional conceptions of merit would discriminate against qualified African-Americans, but what approach to selection would be fairer? Job candidates are best protected against discriminatory standards if a broad range of criteria is used. Minorities, because they score lower on average than whites on some standardized tests[59] and have lower average high school and college grades,[60] will be hurt if exclusively traditional qualifications are used, or if institutions consider some of those qualifications definitive. Hiring and promoting criteria should include references from multiple sources, which demonstrate specific ability and skills that are reasonably related to the job in question. A broader range of qualifications also includes some indicators of potential job success, such as internships, apprenticeships, or past work experience. This approach to discerning is fairer to applicants because it does not pin their chances for selection solely on a test score or GPA.

Higher education admissions must also use many criteria when trying to predict academic success. As shown, if SAT scores and/or high school rank or grades are the controlling qualifications for undergraduate admissions, significant numbers of qualified African-Americans will not be admitted. College selection committees can evaluate applicants through multiple references, which estimate academic potential, and should consider students' personal and economic situations, which may have contributed to underperformance in high school. Colleges should also conduct student interviews, which can be structured to discern motivation, interest in subject areas, and intelligence. Writing samples can also be relevant for these purposes.

Using a broad range of criteria to discern academic or job skill potential ensures that African-Americans will be given a fair look in the selection process, but race must also be added to the list of relevant qualifications. Affirmative action is a legitimate attempt by government and private-sector institutions to decrease racial stereotypes and to encourage African Americans to pursue their life goals. This implies that the negative prejudgments of blacks by employers, college admissions officers, and others, may deter the upward mobility of blacks. These forms of discrimination can best be attacked through affirmative action hiring and admissions programs. These policies will also decrease black discouragement, which is exacerbated by frequent encounters with racism. Although race does not prejudge potentiality, selecting qualified blacks demonstrates to others that hard work and perseverance can pay-off, and black successes help to break down stereotypes in peers as well as in super-ordinates.[61] Race is a legitimate merit because of the social purposes selecting qualified blacks, who would not be considered if tests and GPA were controlling qualifications, helps to achieve. Evidence for the persistence of racist stereotypes and discrimination is discussed in the following section.

PERSISTENT RACIAL DISCRIMINATION

The defense of affirmative action presented so far has focused primarily on merit, but present racial discrimination must be added. The following studies suggest that stereotyping and discrimination exist in many areas of American life. White racial attitudes reveal a significant amount of prejudice toward African-Americans. A survey conducted by the National Opinion Research Center (NORC), found that 52 percent of whites believe that racial inequality is due to a lack of motivation on the part of African-Americans.[62] Other surveys revealed that 65 percent of whites feel that blacks are lazier than whites.[63] Whites tend to rate themselves as more self-supporting and harder-working than blacks,[64] and 75 percent of whites feel blacks should try harder to achieve equality.[65] Racial stereotypes regarding African-American behavior and intellectual ability also persist. A national Race Survey found that 52 percent of whites think blacks are aggressive or violent,[66] and a General Social Survey (GSS) found that whites tend to rate themselves as less violence prone than blacks.[67] A GSS survey revealed that 56 percent of whites[68] believe blacks to be less intelligent than whites, and that whites tend to feel themselves to be more intelligent than blacks.[69] Given the persistence of whites' negative attitudes toward African-Americans it is not surprising that the GSS finds that about 50 percent of Western European Americans and about 55 percent of Eastern European Americans object to living in a neighborhood which is about 50 percent black.[70] An Institute for Survey Research (ISR) poll found that 43 percent of whites desire to live in a mostly white or all white neighborhood.[71] Also not surprising is a NORC survey which reveals that 49 percent of whites object to sending their children to schools where more than half the student population is black.[72]

Further evidence for the claim that race is still an influential factor in American society, one that can have negative repercussions for African-Americans, is seen in other studies. An Urban League Study found that blacks are denied housing loans 60 percent more often than whites, and blacks paid higher interest rates than whites on such loans.[73] A previous study of racial differences in mortgage lending revealed that black applicants were denied mortgages at twice the rate of whites.[74] A study conducted by the department of Housing and Urban Development (HUD), found that 22 percent of prospective black renters, and 17 percent of prospective black home buyers faced discrimination.[75]

Various studies suggest that racial discrimination in hiring is not a marginal practice. A study of hiring in the Washington, D.C. and Chicago, Illinois metropolitan areas reported that ". . . blacks receive unfavorable differential treatment 20 percent of the time they compete against comparable whites for entry-level positions."[76] This finding is particularly compelling since all of the black job applicants were over-qualified for the positions that they sought and ". . . were articulate . . ., dressed conventionally, and posed as having prior job experience."[77] Other studies corroborate the hiring study. A national study of over four-thousand employers from a widely representative sample of jobs conducted by Jomills Braddock and James McPartland found that, for jobs which required verbal skills, mathematical skills, and high school degrees, employers avoided hiring blacks. These researchers also found that "statistical discrimination" is often a significant problem for blacks who have not completed a college degree, and in ". . . lower-level jobs when academic and learning traits are highly valued."[78] Statistical discrimination involves the use of group identifiers, such as race, in hiring decisions. It occurs when employers use negative stereotypes to predict how applicants from different racial-groups will perform the jobs they seek. Braddock and McPartland also found "information bias" against minorities—employers' tendency to be more suspect of applicant information provided by minority firms, schools, or clergy. Joleen Kirschenman and Kathryn M. Neckerman found that Chicago area employers often held negative views of the potential of inner-city black men to become competent workers. They concluded that, "[r]ace is an important factor in hiring decisions . . ." because most of the employers who were interviewed ". . . associated negative images with . . . black men" and "whether through skills tests, credentials, personal references, folk theories, or their intuition . . . [employers] used some means of screening out the inner-city applicant."[79] These selection decisions were often motivated by negative bias about the productivity of inner-city black men. Bolstering the evidence for racial hiring discrimination is the federal government's Glass Ceiling Commission study. The study found that ninety-seven percent of senior managers in the top one-thousand United States industrial companies and the five-hundred biggest companies of all types are white, and that this was partially a result of ". . . persistent stereotyping . . ."of blacks.[80] The commission revealed that because of racial prejudice, many companies assigned blacks to jobs in personnel, research, or administration that did not lead to many upper-level positions. A five year study of four major U.S. cities, sponsored by the Russell Sage Foundation, and the Harvard University Multi-disciplinary Program in Inequality and Social Policy, found pervasive negative stereotyping of blacks by employers.[81] The continuing incidence of racism and hiring discrimination against African-Americans is not surprising in light of the previously discussed public opinion studies. These studies and surveys suggest that hiring discrimination and racism persist in the United States. These findings contradict the contentions of affirmative action critics, such as Stephan Thernstrom and Abigail Thernstrom, who argue that racism and discrimination have largely disappeared.[82]

COMBINING A CRITIQUE OF MERIT WITH OTHER AFFIRMATIVE ACTION DEFENSES

Preventing or attempting to counteract present racial discrimination is, by itself, a compelling defense of affirmative action in employment, given the variety and wide-ranging characteristic of the studies discussed in this section. However, concerns about qualifications, the crux of affirmative action opposition, are effectively addressed by thinking about merit in a rational way. The realities of affirmative action successes in hiring, higher education and public contracts, which demonstrate the viability of using a broad range of selection criteria dispels the assumptions of the validity of assigning controlling influence to one or two qualifications. Accordingly, present racial discrimination and the debunking of narrow views of merit work in tandem in the defense of affirmative action in employment presented here.

The goal of diversifying American institutions, itself, is also a compelling defense of affirmative action programs. The benefits of diversity are documented in a number of studies. A.W. Astin surveyed nearly 25,000 students from 217 colleges over a four year period and concluded that students expressed greater awareness of other cultures, increased understanding of other races, more satisfaction with campus life and benefits for critical thinking, problem-solving and writing skills, because of racially diverse student bodies.[83] E.T. Pascarella et. al, found that white college students who took advantage of diversity efforts on campus developed racial awareness that was similar to that of students of color.[85] Similar to a defense of affirmative action based solely on present racial discrimination, the diversity emphasis is strengthened against concerns about qualifications by adding a rational critique of merit to the defense. In other words, diversity goals can legitimately be accomplished when colleges and employers use a broad mix of selection criteria, and affirmative action successes put to rest reverse discrimination claims.

The argument that affirmative action is justified because of past racial discrimination is akin to the diversity defense of the policy. One can attribute the lack of African-Americans in particular corporate positions, as shown in the Glass Ceiling Commission study, to continuing as well as past discrimination. However, the remedy for the dearth of blacks in certain corporate jobs is to diversify; but again the past discrimination defense must include a rational critique of merit to allay concerns about qualifications.

DEBUNKING THE SELF-RESPECT CRITIQUE

The successes of affirmative action counter the reverse discrimination claim of its critics. But the critique of reified views of merit also attacks the argument that affirmative action decreases its beneficiaries self-respect.[85] Empirical evidence, on the whole, suggests that any negative effects on blacks' self-respect or self-worth from affirmative action is far outweighed by its positive outcomes. A 1995 Gallup poll found that 81 percent of African-American women and 71 percent of African-American men did not question their abilities because of affirmative action.[86] M.C. Taylor analyzed responses on the 1990 GSS survey, and concluded that black men who were employed by firms that used affirmative action were more ambitious than those who worked in businesses that did not participate in affirmative action.[87] A Catalyst study of U.S. corporations revealed that female African-American employees saw affirmative action programs as helping them to be rewarded for their merit.[88] K. Truax, et al, found that while 60 percent of black undergraduates believed that their peers doubted their abilities, and 50 percent believed that their professors did, over two-thirds of the black students did not doubt themselves.[89]

These studies, along with the achievements of affirmative action beneficiaries previously shown, and the long term African-American support for the policy[90] provide a strong sense that most blacks' self-respect and self-worth have not been damaged. The Bok and Bowen study found that thirty-three percent of blacks with doctorates have led community and social activities. Twenty-one, eighteen, and fourteen percent, respectively, of blacks with law, medical, and business degrees have also been leaders of civic activities.[91] These blacks, as Bok and Bowen argue, ". . . serve as strong threads in a fabric that binds their own community together and binds those communities into the larger social fabric . . ."[92] Bok and Bowen imply that successful

African-Americans are role models as well as invaluable sources of information for other blacks who wish to learn the pathways to achieving personal goals. No one could plausibly suggest that these blacks, most of whom are affirmative action beneficiaries, have low self-esteem or suffer debilitating self-doubt. The professional and civic contributions that affirmative action beneficiaries have made demonstrate that race-conscious programs are worth the risk of some possible self-questioning.

Traditional preferences, in creating opportunities for whites, have not caused them to decrease their efforts to advance economically. Indeed, white ethnic groups have used urban political machines to get municipal jobs and city contracts throughout most of the 20th century. Douglas Massey and Nancy Denton point out that patronage allowed white ethnic groups to get a foothold in the working-class, from which they advanced further.[93] For Irish, Italians, Jews, and Poles, patronage was integral to economic mobility.[94] But these opportunities did not produce a mass of unmotivated and self-doubting individuals. If their self-confidence had been hurt, such groups would not have achieved a better quality of life. Whites, in short, took advantage of patronage and worked hard to move up. It is hard to argue that these white ethnics did not know *why* they were hired or awarded public contracts. Yet such knowledge did not create a widespread or significant diminution of self-respect. Similarly, the success of affirmative action beneficiaries suggest that many African-Americans have used affirmative action to advance without significant damage to self-confidence.

Affirmative action in college admissions policies provided blacks, who are now professionals, with opportunities for individual achievement. Higher education affirmative action programs often admit racial minorities who have lower test scores and grades than whites. Had they not, many of the blacks who became professionals would not have, absent race as one of many valid admissions criteria. The assumed objectivity of tests and grades needs qualification, and such unanalyzed beliefs are central to the self-respect critique. If many of these successful blacks had been solely evaluated according to traditional views of merit, which rank-order applicants based on test scores and grades, many Americans would have regarded them as poor risks to succeed. But since some *do* succeed, such narrow views of qualifications have to be re-evaluated and expanded. As I have argued, race is a morally compelling selection criterion because it decreases racial stereotypes and provides role models. But race is only one valid criterion among others. Valid tests and grades are also legitimate components of an evaluation process, but should not be exclusively definitive. The claim that affirmative action decreases blacks' incentives and rigorous self-application is significantly weakened when broader views of merit are understood. How could the impressive

achievements of African-Americans, over the last three decades, which required individual effort, have been achieved by persons consumed by self
doubt and who are less qualified?

TRADITIONAL PREFERENCES AS SEGUES

Traditional preferences do not provoke the charge that they lower whites'
self-respect.[95] This argument deepens the debate over affirmative action policy. Traditional preferences have never been controversial. Traditional preferences do not consider test scores and grades to be controlling qualifications.
But this has never been a hotly debated public issue, as it is in the affirmative
action controversies. Other types of criteria, such as Veterans service, financial contributions from academic legacies, political support and votes from
patronage beneficiaries, and athletic ability, are largely accepted by Americans, and race, as one of several selective criteria, is as morally, if not more
so, compelling as these others. Adding race to the mix of socially or institu-
tionally important qualifications may seem fairer to Americans if it is argued
within this context, and just as important is the fact that traditional preferences can make Americans accept a broader meaning of merit. If athletes'
preferences are worth the risk of self-doubt, and traditional preferences are
not so concerned with traditional criteria, then allowing blacks, who may also
have lower traditional credentials, the opportunity to achieve goals seems, at
least, equally viable, both socially and morally. Race, as one valid selection
criteria among others, becomes more morally compelling here.

SUMMARY

This chapter has attempted to provide a more compelling defense of affirmative action than those given, historically, by high-profile and other political
elites, as discussed in chapter one. The following chapter analyzes the arguments for class-based affirmative action and similar policies from the rational
critique of merit perspective.

NOTES

1. Jomills Henry Braddock II and James M. Partland, "How Minorities Continue
to be Excluded from Equal Employment Opportunities: Research on Labor Market
and Institutional Barriers,"*Journal of Social Issues*, Vol. 43, 1, (1987): Appendix.

2. See Infra notes 62–81 and accompanying text.

3. See Peter Dreier and Regina Freer, "Saints, Sinners, and Affirmative Action," in *The Chronicles of* Higher Education, October 24, 1997, B6–B7; *Philadelphia Inquirer*, December 7, 2001, G10; *Philadelphia Inquirer*, June 24, 2003, A8; *Philadelphia Inquirer*, June 28, 2003, A7.

4. 401 U.S. 424 (1971) at 433.

5. *Philadelphia Inquirer*, November 30, 2002, A10.

6. *Philadelphia Inquirer*, May 15, 2002, A5

7. Ibid.

8. *Philadelphia Inquirer,* August 29, 2003, A2.

9. *Philadelphia Inquirer,* May 15, 2002, A5.

10. *Philadelphia Inquirer*, December 7, 2001, G10.

11. 78F.3d932 (5th Cir. 1996).

12. Ibid. at 935, n.2 and 563.

13. Ibid. at 563, n.32.

14. Theodore Cross, "What If There Was No Affirmative Action in College Admissions? A Further Refinement of Our Earlier Conclusions,"in *The Journal of Blacks in Higher Education*, No. 5, (Autumn, 1994): pp.52–55.

15. Ibid., pp. 54–55.

16. James Crouse and Dale Trusheim, *The Case Against the SAT* (Chicago: The University of Chicago Press, 1988), p.105.

17. Ibid.

18. William G. Bowen and Derek Bok, *The Shape of the River: Long-Term Consequences of Considering Race in College and University Admissions* (Princeton, N.J.: Princeton University Press: 1998), p.282.

19. Ibid., p.104–105.

20. Cross, "What If There Was No Affirmative Action,"pp.54–55.

21. Robert C. Davidson and Ernest L. Lewis, "Affirmative Action and Other Special Consideration Admissions at the University of California, Davis School of Medicine,"in *Journal of the American Medical Association*, 278, (1997): pp. 1153–1158.

22. Robert Klitgaard, *Choosing Elites* (New York: Basic Books, 1985), p.155.

23. Andrew Hacker, *Two Nations* (New York: Charles Scribner's Sons, 1992), p.98.

24. Bok and Bowen, *The Shape of the River*, pp. 37–38.

25. Ibid., p.45.

26. Ibid., p.57.

27. Linda F. Wightman, "The Threat to Diversity in Legal Education: An Empirical Analysis of the Consequences of Abandoning Race as a Factor in Law School Admissions Decisions," *New York University Law Review*, 72, 1, (1997): pp.4–5, 36.

28. Ibid., p.28.

29. Davidson and Lewis, "Affirmative Action and Other Special Considerations Admissions," p. 1156.

30. Crouse and Trusheim, *The Case Against the SAT*, p.105.

31. Bok and Bowen, *The Shape of the River*, pp.112–113.

32. Ibid., p.116.

33. 401 U.S. 424 (1971) at 431.

34. Ibid., at 431–432.

35. John A. Hartigan and Alexandra K. Wigdor, eds., *Fairness in Employment Testing* (Washington, D.C.: National Academy Press, 1989), p.42.

36. Ibid., pp.258–260.

37. Alexandra K. Wigdor and Bert F. Green, Jr., eds., *Performance Assessment for the Workplace*, Volume 1 (Washington, D.C.: National Academy Press, 1991), p.179.

38. Henry Holzer and David Neumark, "Are Affirmative Action Hires Less Qualified? Evidence from Employer-Employee Data on New Hires,"*Journal of Labor Economics*, Vol.17, 3,(1999), p.557.

39. Ibid, p. 564–567.

40. Liz McMillen, "Policies Said to Help Companies Hire Qualified Workers at No Extra Cost," *The Chronicle of Higher Education*, November 17, 1995, A7.

41. Jonathan S. Leonard, "The Impact of Affirmative Action on Employment," *Journal of Labor Economics*, Volume 2, 4, (October, 1984): pp.439–463.

42. Ibid.

43. Nicholas P. Lovrich, Jr., Brent S. Steel, and David Hood, "Equity Versus Productivity: Affirmative Action and Municipal Police Forces," *Public Productivity Review*, 39, (!986): pp 65-69.

44. Ibid.

45. 448 U.S. 448 (1980) at 407.

46. Timothy Bates, *Banking on Black Enterprise* (Washington, D.C.: Joint Center for Political and Economic Studies, 1993), p. 94.

47. *Philadelphia Inquirer*, May 7, 1997, A6.

48. *Philadelphia Inquirer*, April 11, 1994, A2.

49. George R. La Noue, "Split Visions: Minority Business Set-Asides," in *The Annals of the American Academy of Political and Social Science*, Vol. 523, eds., Harold Orlans and June O'Neil (Newbury Park: SAGE Publications, Inc., 1992), p.110.

50. Farrell Bloch, *Antidiscrimination Law and Minority Employment* (Chicago: The University of Chicago Press, 1994), p.127.

51. Gerald Jaynes and Robin Williams, eds., *A Common Destiny: Blacks and American Society* (Washington, D.C.: National Academy Press, 1989), p. 250.

52. Bates, *Banking on Black Enterprise*, p.101.

53. Ibid., p.140.

54. Ibid.

55. John David Skrentny, *The Ironies of Affirmative Action* (The University of Chicago Press, 1996), p.27.

56. 401 U.S. 424 (1971) at 433.

57. On this point I have been aided by Michael Walzer. See Michael Walzer, *Spheres of Justice* (New York: Basic Books, 1983), pp.135–146.

58. Ibid.

59. Supra notes, 14–21, 24, 35.

60. Supra notes, 29–32.

61. On these points regarding the benefits of diversity, I have been aided by Ronald Dworkin. See Ronald Dworkin, "Are Quotas Unfair?," in *Racial Preference*

and Racial Justice, Russell Nieli, Ed. (Washington D.C.: Ethics and Public Policy Center,1991), pp.175–189.

62. Howard Schuman et. al., *Racial Attitudes in America: Trends and Interpretations* (Cambridge, Mass. and London, England: Harvard University Press, 1997), p.157.

63. George E. Peterson and Wayne P. Vroman, "Urban Labor Markets and Economic Opportunity," in *Urban Labor Markets and Job Opportunity,* eds., George E. Peterson and Wayne P. Vroman (Washington D.C.: Urban Institute Press, 1992), p.18.

64. Steven A. Tuch and Jack K. Martin, eds., *Racial Attitudes in the 1990s: Continuity and Change* (Westport, Connecticut: Praeger, 1997), pp.98–104.

65. Schuman et. al., *Racial Attitudes*, pp.156–157, 163.

66. Paul M. Sniderman and Thomas Piazza, *The Scar of Race* (Cambridge, Mass.: Harvard University Press, 1993), p.45.

67. Tuch and Martin, *Racial Attitudes*, p. 100.

68. Peterson and Vroman, *Urban Labor Markets*, p.18.

69. Tuch and Martin, *Racial Attitudes*, p.101.

70. Ibid., pp. 126–133.

71. Schuman et. al., *Racial Attitudes*, pp.100–101.

72. Ibid., pp.140–141.

73. *Philadelphia Inquirer*, July 31, 1998, A10.

74. *Philadelphia Inquirer*, August 5, 1997, C1.

75. *Philadelphia Inquirer*, November 8, 2002, A17.

76. Margery Austin Turner et. al., *Opportunities Denied, Opportunities Diminished* (Washington, D.C.: The Urban Institute Press, 1991), p.61.

77. Ibid.

78. Braddock and McPartland, "How Minorities Continue to Be Excluded," Appendix.

79. Joleen Kirschenman and Kathryn M. Neckerman, "We'd Love to Hire Them, But . . .: The Meaning of Race for Employers," in *The Urban Underclass*, eds. Christopher Jencks and Paul E. Peterson (Washington, D.C.: Brookings Institution, 1991), pp.204–231, 208.

80. *Philadelphia Inquirer*, March 16, 1995, A1, A8.

81. *Philadelphia Inquirer*, October 2, 1999, A1, A7.

82. Stephan and Abigail Thernstrom, *America in Black and White* (New York: Simon and Schuster, 1997)

83. Bettina C. Shuford, "Recommendations for the Future" in *Responding to the New Affirmative Action Climate*, ed., Donald D. Gehring (San Francisco: Jossey-Bass Publishers, 1998), p.73.

84. Ibid.

85. What I refer to as the self-respect critique of affirmative action can be found in the following work: Thomas Sowell, "Are Quotas Good for Blacks," in Nieli, *Racial Preference and Racial Justice*, pp.417–428; Glenn Loury, "Beyond Civil Rights,"in Nieli, *Racial Preference and Racial Justice*, pp.437–451; Albert G. Mosely and Nicholas Capaldi, *Affirmative Action* (New York: Rowman and Littlefield, Inc., 1996), pp.92–109.

86. Cited in Faye J. Crosby, Bernardo Ferdman, and Blanche R. Wingate, "Addressing and Redressing Discrimination: Affirmative Action in Social Psychological Perspective," in *Sex, Race, and Merit: Debating Affirmative Action in Education and Employment* (Ann Arbor: The University of Michigan Press: 2000), p.135.

87. Ibid., 135–136.

88. Ibid., 135.

89. Ibid., 136.

90. See, The Gallup Poll (Wilmington, Delaware: Scholarly Resources, Inc., 1995), p.44, 228 and Seymour Martin Lipset, "Equal Chances versus Equal Results," in *The Annals of The American Academy of Political and Social Science*, Orlans and O'Neill, p.67.

91. *New York Times*, September 9, 1998, B10.

92. Ibid.

93. Douglas S. Massey and Nancy A. Denton, *American Apartheid: Segregation and the Making of the Underclass* (Cambridge, Mass.: Harvard University Press, 1993), pp.154-155.

94. Thomas Byrne Edsall and Mary D. Edsall, *Chain Reaction* (New York: W.W. Norton, 1992), p.254.

95. See Gertrude Ezorsky, Racism and Justice (Ithaca, New York: Cornell University Press, 1991), pp.93–94 and Barbara Bergman, *In Defense of Affirmative Action* (New York: Basic Books, 1996), pp.118–125, 139–141.

Chapter Three

The Class-Based Argument

Some critics of race-based affirmative action have argued that it should be based solely on class disadvantage. Richard Kahlenberg claims that class-based policy is fair because class disadvantage obscures academic and professional potential in some lower-class and working-class individuals of all races.[1] Kahlenberg also argues that middle-class minorities are less disadvantaged than lower and working-class people of all races, and therefore should not benefit from affirmative action. A view similar to Kahlenberg's is expressed by Harold Hodgkinson. Hodgkinson points out that race-based affirmative action obscures that "one quarter of black households have higher incomes than the average white household."[2] To Kahlenberg, a class-based affirmative action policy has the potential to decrease whites' resentment of affirmative action, and to build a cross-racial political coalition, which is necessary to increase popular support for programs that expand social welfare and ensure economic security.[3] Gary Pavela corroborates Kahlenberg, though Pavela does not advocate eliminating race from affirmative action, by doubting that colleges and universities can maintain support for affirmative action unless class considerations become a plus in the admissions process.[4]

Kahlenberg argues that the claimed "level playing field" is not so level. He cites a study by Gary Solon, which found that males who are born into the bottom five percent of the economic distribution have a 50-percent chance of remaining there, a 25-percent chance of rising above the average, and a 5-percent chance of making the top fifth.[5] White working-class children grow up in families where economic survival and a non-violent family atmosphere is sought, but where intellectual stimulation, reading, and communication are not encouraged.[6] Kahlenberg points out that SAT scores decline as family income declines; the average combined SAT score for children whose parents make seventy thousand dollars a year is 234 points higher than those of children whose families make ten thousand dollars annually. The average combined SAT score of children whose families earn seventy thousand dollars per year is 144 points higher than the average score of the children whose families make twenty thousand dollars annually.[7] Children's academic achievement is also highly correlated with parental education; children are more likely to attend college if a parent had.[8] The lack of equal education funding, exemplified by the frequent large gaps in per-pupil expenditure between poor and wealthy school districts, and the increased at-risk factors of lower-class children in regards to drugs, violence, and dropping out, demonstrate the class-bias in educational opportunity.[9] One basis of Kahlenberg's argument, class disadvantage may hide academic potential, implicitly critiques traditional conceptions of merit. Why admit a lower-class or working class applicant with a sub-par SAT score into college if he or she is not thought to be qualified? Kahlenberg advocates admitting such applicants,[10] so he must not believe that a strict rank ordering of applicants based on test scores and grades is fair or legitimate. An argument that implies a critique of traditional merit views cannot be against race considerations in affirmative action. The following section will show why such considerations are necessary for middle-class African-Americans.

SHOULD MIDDLE-CLASS MINORITIES BENEFIT FROM AFFIRMATIVE ACTION?

Higher Education

Eliminating race preferences in higher education would be unfair. According to Crouse and Trusheim, if colleges base admissions solely on high school rank, nearly thirteen percent of blacks who could earn a bachelor's degree will be rejected. If admissions are based on high school rank and SAT scores, more than twenty-two percent of blacks who can graduate will be rejected.[11] Crouse and Trusheim derived these figures by looking at the percentages of African-Americans who earned a bachelor's degree despite SAT scores and grades that were below the normal cut-offs of many colleges. If such admissions cut-offs had been employed, thousands of African-Americans would be unfairly rejected annually. Considering the increases in the black middle-class since 1970, as of 1997 thirty-two percent of males and nearly sixty percent of females are presently in middle-class occupations,[12] and nationally 50 percent of black college matriculants are poor and 3 percent are wealthy, leaving many in the middle class.[13] Some middle-class blacks would be among this rejected group, and some would be hurt by class-based affirmative action in higher education. Absent racial considerations in affirmative action, which lowers the bar on SAT and grade requirements, or considers them as two of many criteria, some more qualified middle-class blacks would be rejected; the average middle class black's combined SAT scores are nearly 160 points lower than those of middle-class whites,[14] even those admitted to selective schools,[15] and have lower average grades. The average middle-class black's combined SAT score is also lower than the average lower class white's.[16] Therefore, if such scores and GPA are given inordinate weight in determining which applicants are admitted, some middle-class blacks who have academic potential will be rejected.

Current academic selection strategies further the point that middle-income blacks are hurt when test scores are too influential in the admissions process. Colleges have recently been focusing on recruitment efforts in the suburbs. As a result, selection criteria put more weight on the SAT and GPA, and even high-scoring students, because of increased competition, seek admission to less selective schools, leaving lower scoring applicants (many of the economic disadvantaged and for African-Americans many middle-class applicants) at a distinct disadvantage.[17]

The test scores and grades-gap between middle-class blacks and whites demands that public education from elementary to high-school devote considerable resources to repairing African-Americans' education. However, racial and cultural differences may be partly responsible for middle class blacks' poorer (on average) performance. Public education programs should address the cultural factors that may hurt African-Americans' academic performance. Such programs can help black students identify why a given attitude, behavior, or other cultural orientation may ill-serve African-American progress. These programs can also suggest new orientations that aim to achieve better test scores and grades. Even middle-class blacks still often live in segregated communities, attend inferior schools, and may be the first generation in their families to have experienced significant upward mobility. As a result of these structural conditions, middle-class blacks may not have been exposed to high educational standards and expectations. Christopher Jencks and Meredith Phillips point out that the educational gaps between blacks and whites typically begin before first grade.[18] This suggests that there are strong structural, social, familial and cultural forces responsible for these gaps. Middle-class and upper-class whites are more likely to have been exposed to higher academic expectations and are often better prepared for academic achievement. This is not to argue that all middle-class white college applicants should be evaluated for admissions solely on traditional criteria. But the structural advantages that middle-class whites have, compared to the barriers that middle-class African-Americans face, which could well be responsible for their lower test scores and grades, but which mask academic potential, argue that non-traditional qualifications be given more weight, especially given society's need for racial diversity.

Employment

If employment tests are given definitive power in hiring and promoting, African-Americans of all classes will be hurt because blacks, on average, do worse on such tests than whites do.[19] But the *Griggs* and *Albemarle* Supreme Court cases, and the National Research Council Studies on employment tests discussed in chapter two, demonstrate that such tests may have adverse impact on African-Americans. However, the need to maintain race considerations in hiring and promoting becomes more imperative when one considers that racism and racial discrimination persist in American society. As discussed in chapter two, a national study by Jomills Henry Braddock II and James M. McPartland reveals that employers use negative predictions about black job performance in selection processes and are suspicious of black applicants' references when they come from black sources. Both of these phenomena were found to result in hiring discrimination.[20] The federal government's Glass Ceiling Commission reported that ". . . persistent stereotyping . . ." is a causal factor in the small percentages of African-Americans who are corporate senior managers.[21]

The Braddock and McPartland study looked at a nationally representative sample of jobs , and the Glass Ceiling Commission study sampled most major American corporations. This shows that middle-class blacks confront present discrimination. Race considerations in affirmative action, which attempt to decrease hiring discrimination by making employers aware of the tendency to stereotype and prejudge African-Americans, remain necessary; racial hiring goals increase the efforts of employers to challenge these tendencies.

That middle-class blacks earn more income than working class blacks does not protect them from stereotypes. Middle-class blacks may use black English, (although they may be less likely to do this than lower class blacks and working-class blacks) or different communication styles than middle-class whites. Such differences in style can impede their interviews and promotions.[22] Douglass Massey and Nancy Denton argue that employers associate Black English with a lack of "good worker" behaviors, such as "...regularity, punctuality, dependability, and respect for authority.[23] Likewise, Joleen Kirschenmann and Kathryn M. Neckerman find that black speech patterns connote, to white employers, an undesirable worker.[24] While Massey and Denton and Kirshenmann and Neckerman study mainly lower-class blacks, middle-class blacks also often live in segregated neighborhoods, go to segregated schools, and have social contact, predominately with other blacks.[25] The relative higher income of middle class African Americans does not preclude cultural traits, such as speech patterns, that may cause a white employer to prejudge them as unqualified or less qualified. But if communication styles are irrelevant to job performance, these prejudgments are discriminatory. The assumption that an applicant who uses Black English will not perform capably is unfair and can lead to discrimination. Culturally determined communication styles, such as assertive, loud, or demonstrative speaking and bodily movements, are not impediments to successful job performance. Determinations of relevancy depend on the job context. Middle-class white clientele and co-workers may be turned off by unfamiliar communication styles.

Therefore, employees of all races should receive training in institutional expectation and cultural differences. Such training can save a capable minority worker from not being hired or promoted. Institutions must recognize and work with cultural differences. A National Treasury Employee Union study finds that the greater likelihood of black public sector employees to be fired or disciplined is attributable to cultural differences.[26] Employers must determine what personal traits and styles are truly necessary job qualifications. This can only be initiated through a public debate about necessary qualifications. Such a public discussion must aim to counter the persistent belief in traditional notions of selection criteria. Institutions that do not select, or that fire or fail to hire or promote a qualified African-American due to irrelevant cultural differences, or that do so in contexts where employee adjustments to institutional norms are possible, are guilty of discrimination. Affirmative action guidelines require that qualifications be job-related,[27] but public affirmative action proponents must focus on this premise to encourage employers to establish fair criteria selection.

Orlando Patterson claims that affirmative action attempts to help African-Americans learn the ". . . language and culture of power . . ."[28] by helping them get into American educational and workplace institutions. But middle-class blacks cannot readily learn the requirements for employment success if affirmative action is solely class-based, because few will get in the door. Middle-class African-Americans will fail to be exposed to the knowledge vital to success in mainstream American culture if traditional selection criteria are the definitive standards. If race preferences are eliminated in hiring and promotions, the dearth of African-Americans in private sector upper-level positions may well increase. The 1991 Glass Ceiling Commission blames these low percentages on negative racial stereotypes and on the smaller number of blacks in the type of corporate jobs required to advance into upper-level positions.[29] The commission finds few blacks in the sales, production, and marketing positions that often lead to upper-level jobs. Not surprisingly, the few blacks in top-level positions work mainly in human resources, administration, or research, where upward mobility is limited. If race preferences for middle-class blacks are abolished in entry-level private-sector jobs, their numbers in upper-level positions would further decrease since fewer would "get in the door." Companies would also feel less pressure to promote their African-American employees. If affirmative action were solely class-based, the growth of the black middle class would be threatened. A return to traditional hiring and promoting methods, especially in the public sector, where many blacks work, [30] would hurt their chances for upward mobility. Attempts by conservatives to shrink the public sector exacerbates the vulnerability of the African-American middle class. The Glass Ceiling Commission found that ". . . advanced degrees . . . are now considered a prerequisite for climbing the corporate ladder."[31] The attacks on public sector affirmative action, such as Proposition 209, Proposition 200 in Washington, rollbacks in Florida and Georgia,[32] and the successful referendum in Michigan threaten opportunities for all blacks to obtain the credentials required to advance in both private and public institutions. But maintaining racial considerations in affirmative action strengthens the chances for the reproduction—and potential expansion—of the recently created black middle class.

PROBLEMS OF CLASS-BY-ITSELF

A strictly class-based affirmative action policy for higher education would hurt lower-class African-Americans. Although 50 percent of black college matriculants come from lower-class backgrounds versus 22 percent of whites,[33] whites outnumber blacks in the general population by roughly 6 to 1. Clearly the pool of white lower-class applicants is much greater than for blacks since the overall percentages of the two groups attending college is 46 percent for whites and 40 percent for blacks.[34] The situation becomes more ominous when one considers, as discussed in the previous section, that colleges are focusing recruitment on the suburbs and therefore are becoming more selective with traditional criteria. Adding to this potential dilemma for African-Americans is the advantage that formerly middle-class white applicants, who became lower-class through divorce, would receive by attending middle-class schools and doing better on the SAT.[35] Again, merit conceptions would be crucial here i.e. if class became the only consideration and the focus on solely traditional criteria remains intact with class being only a plus, a la the *Bakke* argument, colleges would favor the lower-class applicants with the slightly higher GPA and test scores, many of whom are white. The problems posed by class-based affirmative action in higher education, though based on a study of very selective colleges, but applicable to all are summed up by William G. Bowen and Derek Bok, ". . . there are almost six times as many white students as black students who both come from low-SES families and have test scores that are above the threshold for gaining admission to an academically selective college or university."[36]

WHY CLASS CONSIDERATIONS ARE NECESSARY

For the last two decades, affirmative action has been a major wedge issue, dividing black and white working-class and middle-class Americans.[37] Both Ronald Reagan and George Bush facilitated white working-class and middle-class Democrats' flight from the Democratic Party by opposing racial "quotas" in hiring and higher education.[38] The California electorate's passing of the California Civil Rights Initiative (CCRI), which ended public sector affirmative action in California, was aided by white working-class and middle-class resentment of race-based policies. In November 1998, voters in the state of Washington eliminated public sector affirmative action by a fifty-eight to forty-two percent margin.[39] However, a solely class-based affirmative action would leave middle-class African-Americans virtually unprotected from racial discrimination and unfair selection procedures. At the same time, lower-class and working-class whites do not start the race for material comfort on a level playing field. Fairness and moral consistency require that *all* disadvantaged members of society be given incentives and the chance to develop their talents. In the following analysis, I will argue that a class component must be added to racial considerations for affirmative action policy to foster equality of opportunity for all disadvantaged Americans.

Disadvantaged whites and Asians who have done fairly well in high school but have sub-par SAT scores, or grades, should be assisted since their potential can be obscured by class disadvantage. Class disadvantages make the potential ability of lower-class and working-class children less visible. As shown in the first section of this chapter SAT scores climb significantly as family income increases. However, Crouse and Trusheim have found that if colleges admit lower-income applicants based on high school grades alone, or by SAT and grades, they will predict freshman-year grades correctly in 56 and 59 percent of cases, respectively. More specifically, Crouse and Trusheim find that as many as 57 per one thousand lower-class college applicants would be unfairly rejected if SAT scores and grades were the controlling qualifications in the higher education admissions process.[40] They base these projections on the number of such students who graduate, yet were admitted with

sub-par traditional qualifications. While the adverse impact of these traditional selection criteria on African-American college applicants would be
nearly four times that of lower-class applicants of all races,[41] thousands of the
latter applicants would still be discriminated against yearly.[42] Clearly, the
SAT and high school grades are not air-tight predictors of low-income students' performance. Another disadvantage of class, which may obscure an applicant's ability is the fact that wealthier families can afford test preparation
courses or tutors for their children, which can improve test scores. Various
studies have found average gains on the SAT ranging from 62 to 110 points
as a result of test coaching or training.[43] Compounding the class biases in the
higher education selection process is the possibility that elite graduate and
professional schools may assume that students from lower-ranked colleges
are less capable. Elite undergraduate programs may perceive that students
from community colleges are less qualified. These biases decrease the
chances of lower and working class applicants to attend elite schools. Considering that such students are so underrepresented in elite institutions, this
assumption may have merit.[44]

   Lower-class students must contend with the class biases in education—
particularly, the pervasive lack of adequate college preparation in high
schools. The Department of Education has found that only 67 percent of
whites, 46 percent of blacks, and 47 percent of Hispanics graduated from
four-year colleges within 6 years.[45] Because college is a gateway for upward
mobility, and some lower-class applicants can be unfairly rejected when traditional selection criteria are treated as definitive, affirmative action in higher
education admissions should include class. But clearly, the first priority for
improving the lives of the least favored should be better academic preparation. However, increased funding and resources for school districts that edu-
cate primarily lower-class and working-class students must be combined with
race-neutral social welfare programs. Economically disadvantaged families
who do not have access to decent health care cannot send their children to
school with an attentive, uncluttered mind. As Kahlenberg points out, some
lower-class children live with frequent physical discomfort that results from
long-delayed medical care.[46] These difficult family environments are exacerbated by structural impediments to economic mobility. The unskilled and
low-skilled parent can be thwarted in attempts to provide for a family by a
lack of day-care and job-training programs, and by having to take jobs that
pay non-livable wages. Certainly, children who grow up in such families are
not exposed to books, stable environments, and intellectual stimulation nearly
as often as the children of middle- and upper-class parents. Working-class
college students must also have greater financial assistance. For such students' need to work while taking a full-time course load markedly decreases

their study time. This only compounds the difficulties of students who enter college less academically prepared to begin with. Increased financial aid to colleges' economically-disadvantaged students would help them catch up.

A class component in affirmative-action hiring programs is also just because such considerations promote equal opportunity. Job candidates from disadvantaged backgrounds may have lower high school or college grades, or lower test scores, than others, but may have done relatively well in college considering the difficult environments and the many barriers that they have overcome. Giving these applicants some favor in the hiring and promoting process, as long as they meet minimal relevant criteria, as explained in chapter two, provides role models and encouragement for others from disadvantaged backgrounds. Such programs also help to defeat negative stereotypes about lower- and working-class individuals, that associates their speech and communication styles with a lack of both intelligence and behavioral sophistication. And they will expose middle-class and upper-class co-workers more often to peers with different styles and modest backgrounds who perform their jobs well.

Public Contracts

Affirmative action programs should also consider class disadvantage in awarding public contracts. Although contract competitors are often not economically disadvantaged, some are competitively disadvantaged by economic and social marginalization. Choosing both qualified businesses who have less capital, and other qualified contractors who hire low-wage workers and raise their wages, can bolster the economic power of lower-class and working-class individuals and communities. As shown in chapter two, minority business enterprises (MBEs), grew by more than 115,000 from 1982 to 1987. MBE programs have improved training, capital, and network opportunities for new MBEs and have encouraged other established businesses to share market potential with them.[47] Depressed white communities will benefit in these same ways if relatively disadvantaged white-owned businesses, and those who do business in such communities, or who hire many lower-income or working-class whites, are added to affirmative-action contract programs.

Businesses which are relatively disadvantaged may be those owned by formerly working-class individuals who want to increase their earnings, but lack the capital required for contract bidding, and are unfamiliar with the competitive contract-awarding process. These situations result from initial economic disadvantage, lack of capital, and living in environments with limited access to pertinent information about contracting. Economically disadvantaged whites and blacks alike suffer from unequal education opportunities and troubled environments that thwart their chances for upward mobility. As of 1998, the Philadelphia, Pennsylvania school district spent 1600 dollars less per pupil, yearly, than the average of 61 school districts in the four surrounding countries.[48] Only a minority of Philadelphia public school students read and write at their prescribed levels, and in some areas nearly 50 percent drop out.[49] An *Education Week* report blamed these deficits on economic segregation, pointing out that 58 percent of Pennsylvania children living in impoverished neighborhoods go to Philadelphia schools. The positive relationship between class and academic and economic achievement is clear, but it constitutes *present* class-discrimination, as well as the effects of past discrimination. Low-income students are hurt by inter-generational poverty, but their unequal opportunities are compounded by a lack of present remedies. For these reasons, the entrepreneurs or burgeoning businesses who face a lack of working capital or unfamiliarity with contract processes, and who operate in, or employ workers from disadvantaged communities, should be given preferences in government contract assignments. Contract preferences for relatively disadvantaged businesses promote equal opportunity by bringing them into the bidding process. Absent preferences, a lack of capital or knowledge of the market will unfairly discriminate against some businesses even though such impediments are not their fault. Entrepreneurs from disadvantaged backgrounds often lack inherited wealth or sufficient capital for business expansion. Government contracts for such enterprises increase the potential for upward mobility, and successful businesses provide disadvantaged communities with jobs, information resources, and role models. Contract preferences for such businesses, therefore, facilitate the breakdown of inter-generational economic inequalities.

This section defends adding class to affirmative action because such considerations are morally fair. A later section will show the pragmatic political benefits of adding a class component to race and gender-based policies. The next section will demonstrate the continuing need for gender considerations in various areas of affirmative action.

GENDER

Higher Education

Affirmative action in higher education needs to acknowledge gender as well as race and class. Stereotypical views of women, which perceive them as poor choices for certain jobs[50] persist in American society. Sexist stereotypes are best attacked when significant numbers of women, who are qualified for these jobs, attain them. Only if higher education institutions combine race, class, and gender considerations with other criteria in their admissions process will they create true equal opportunity. Lower-class, working-class, and middle-class black, Latino, and white women who become professionals, and/or rise to prestigious positions, or who perform well in traditionally male jobs send powerful messages to others who are similarly disadvantaged. And their presence in American institutions attacks racial, class, and gender stereotypes. As with race and class disadvantage, gender should count as a plus in the college and university selection process.

The benefits of gender diversity will not occur unless colleges and professional schools produce an ample pool of graduates. If undergraduate admission decisions use a strict ordinal ranking of applicants according to SAT scores, fewer women will be admitted since men have scored, on average, 56 and 41 points higher than women on the SAT.[51] Despite these SAT gender gaps, women have done as well or better, using GPA as a measure, than men in their freshman year.[52] The need to view SAT scores as only one of many selection criteria is clear, but other traditional admissions practices also disadvantage women. The use of legacy and donor admissions in higher education favors white males. According to Shiela Foster, students admitted with the help of the legacy criteria, many white males, had SAT scores 35 points below those of other students.[53] When one considers the 1995 Glass Ceiling Commission study's finding that among the top 1,000 US industrial corporations and the 500 largest of all US companies 95 to 97 percent of senior managers are male,[54] affirmative action in higher education is necessary to overcome the inordinate influence of traditional preferences and selection criteria to provide an abundant pool of women in the market.

Employment

Gender should be a plus along with other hiring and promoting criteria because of persistent discrimination. The Glass Ceiling Commission attributed the dearth of women in corporate senior managerial positions to stereotyping and fear of change.[55] The Commission also found that the usual jobs which lead to senior manager, marketing, sales, and production, contained few women, and as a result the few women in senior positions tended to be in research, administration, or human resources.[56] The job segregation suggested by the Commission's latter finding appears to be intentional since stereotyping and fear of change are identified as casual factors resulting in the low percentages. However, gender as one of many important hiring and promoting criteria is also justified by a lack of diversity in many occupations.

As of 1997, many blue-collar occupations, such as carpenters, mechanics, masons, and plumbers are more than 98 percent male,[57] and 75 percent of physicians and 73 percent of lawyers are also male.[58] Affirmative action for women attacks two related problems here; the breaking down of negative gender stereotypes and women's earning power. The latter problem, as of 1992, women earned 73 cents to the male dollar, is related to the large percentage of women in lower-paying jobs, such as child care, secretaries, receptionists, clerks, bank tellers, among others.[59] Ronald Dworkin's argument that racially diverse institutions break down stereotypes also applies to gender. Successful women carpenters and senior managers demonstrate that they are capable of performing these and any job, and provide role models and inspiration for females of all ages.

Expanding selection criteria to include gender has increased female representation, and demonstrates that effective job performance has not been compromised. The number of female police officers in the United States increased from less than 2,000 to over 20,000 between 1970–1990.[60] Women also made significant gains in banking, steel, and textiles, as well as in corporations such as AT&T, Xerox, Merck&Co., General Motors, Bank America, all due to affirmative action plans.[61] Additionally, occupational segregation by gender decreased by 20 percent between 1970–1990.[62]

The positive inroads that women have made through affirmative action has not resulted in the hiring of the unqualified or less qualified. Holzer and Neumark found that in a variety of businesses in Atlanta, Chicago, Boston, and Detroit female affirmative action hirees' performance evaluations did not differ from those of non-beneficiaries.[63] Studies by Jonathan Leonard and Nicholas Lovrich, et. al. of, US corporations and Police departments, respectively, found no negative effects on job performance from hiring women. In fact, a study by Hellerstein, Neumark, and Troske concluded that in large plants a positive correlation existed between the number of female employees and stronger performances by the firm.[64]

Public Contracts

Gender considerations in affirmative action policy needs to be included in the allocation of public contracts. In 1979, President Jimmy Carter issued Executive Order 12138, which attempted to discourage discrimination against female entrepreneurs.[65] In 1987 and 1988, federal laws were passed, which, respectively, set gender-based goals for the allocations of federal highway contracts and promoted businesses owned by women.[66] These government acts caused the number of women-owned firms to increase from 2.6 million to 4.1 million between 1982 and 1987,[67] and have also facilitated a significant rise in the share of highway contracts awarded to female-owned construction companies.[68] In 1979, female-owned firms received *zero* federal dollars, but their share of highway contracts alone has increased to 6.7 percent of all federal highway contract expenditures in recent years.[69] Such programs, which allow female-owned businesses to compete in a previously male-dominated bidding process, attack gender stereotypes that restrict job choices for women and encourage them to pursue entrepreneurial opportunities. The proliferation of female-owned firms fosters economic independence in women and increased political power. By accumulating capital and playing prominent roles in local economies, women create a context in which women's issues cannot be ignored by male-dominated power structures. Women may also be more likely than some males to hire other women and to subcontract with female-owned businesses.

OTHER ALTERNATIVES TO RACE-BASED PROGRAMS

Alternatives to race and gender-based affirmative action, besides class considerations, have been tried in Texas, California, and Florida. These states have instituted percent plans for their state university, and California and Texas also consider hardship, overcoming difficulties such as poverty, as one criteria among others.[70] Percent plans, admitting the top 10 percent, for example, of any high school class in a state, is class-like. The current use of economic hardship is essentially a class consideration. Percent plans have been instituted since affirmative action was eliminated in the California public sector, and are used for college admissions in Florida and Texas. These programs intend to create racial diversity while not being overtly race-conscious.

Percent plans have significant drawbacks. In 2000, Texas' program had increased the number of black freshmen at the Flagship campus, University of Texas at Austin, to beyond what it was before the *Hopwood* decision ended affirmative action there.[71] However, the U.S. Commission on Civil Rights reported that the overall percentage of black students admitted to the Austin campus fell from 57 percent of black applicants to 46 percent, while whites remained at 62 percent.[72] Many black applicants who would have been accepted under affirmative action were rejected because they did not fall within the top 10 percent.

The relative success of the Texas plan is contingent on two factors; Texas' high schoolers who are within the 10 percent cut-off can choose to go to the Flagship campus, Austin and the Texas A & M University at College Station, and Texas high schools tend to be racially segregated.[73] The California and Florida plans do not appear to be headed for the same results as Texas. Catherine Horn and Stella Flores found that in 2001–02 black, Native American and urban students were underrepresented, but white, Hispanic and rural students were overrepresented under California's 4 percent program.[74] Similarly,

Patricia Marin and Edgar Lee found that Florida's 20 percent plan benefits whites and Asians more than blacks and Hispanics, due to the overrepresentation of the former and the underrepresentation of the latter in the top 20 percent.[75] As a result of these problems in California and Florida coupled with those who do fall within these state's cut-offs being unable to choose the flagship colleges, a two-tier education system has developed in California and may also in Florida according to the U.S. Commission on Civil Rights; minority students often end up in lower-ranked schools.[76] The Commission also points out that percent plans do not apply to graduate and professional schools,[77] therefore rendering many qualified African-Americans with somewhat lower traditional qualifications, as shown in chapter two, with less opportunities to pursue such degrees.

The pitfalls of percent plans demonstrate that they are inadequate replacements for affirmative action. Such plans do not implicitly acknowledge, as does affirmative action, that a numerical cut-off does not automatically and without fail correctly establish the qualified from the less or unqualified. African-Americans who attend integrated high schools may be qualified for college, but not fall within the 4, 10, or 20 percent of their class.[78] Considering hardship when evaluating lower or working class applicants needs to be coupled with a broader view of merit or black college applicants with lower SAT's or class rank than lower or working class whites or Asians will be denied opportunities and the latter groups could be favored over middle class African-Americans with lower traditional criteria, but who may be qualified to succeed in college.[79]

THE POLITICAL BENEFITS OF A RACE, CLASS, AND GENDER-BASED POLICY

Affirmative action defenders need to argue for a race, class, and gender-based policy for political, as well as moral, reasons. Affirmative action is a wedge issue that divides white and black voters and generates significant political clout for Republican politicians who oppose it. In the 1980 Presidential election, Ronald Reagan, who had made his anti-affirmative action stand a major part of his campaign rhetoric, received the votes of thirty-one percent of Democrats who were opposed to special efforts by government to assist minorities.[80] In the 1980 Presidential election, Reagan also received the vote of seventy-one percent of all voters, who strongly opposed specific government programs to help blacks.[81] George Bush, in the 1988 Presidential election, also had some success in winning the support of conservative Democrats—in part, by opposing "quotas".[82] Proposition 209, which eliminated all public sector affirmative action programs in California, was favored, according to a 1996 Gallup poll, by sixty-one percent of Americans.[83] Also, in a 1995 Gallup poll, sixty-one percent of whites favored such policies, but this figure dropped to nine percent when affirmative action was perceived to involve the use of quotas.[84] Clearly, opposition to affirmative action remains a popular political campaign position in the mind of a majority of American whites. Despite general white opposition to affirmative action, the margin of victory for Proposition 209 was only eight percent.[85] If affirmative action had included lower and working-class whites, its defenders may have prevailed in California. Since affirmative action for women increases support for the policy, both in California[86] and the nation,[87] including class criteria probably would, as well. According to John Donahue, a Northwestern University Law School professor and Clinton Administration affirmative action consultant, people favor government programs if they or someone they know is benefiting from them.[88] Donahue implies that white men are more supportive of affirmative action if they perceive that their wife, mother, or daughter is a recipient. It stands to reason that if lower and working-class white men and their families were included in affirmative action, they would be more likely to support its policies. However, whites' opposition to affirmative action is tied to their perception that government social welfare programs unfairly redistribute income and resources from whites to racial minorities.[89] If class is added to race and gender in affirmative action policy, *and* liberal Democrats and affirmative action proponents also campaign for a universal and broad-based social welfare policy, the wedge between white and black voters may weaken. As William Julius Wilson points out, middle-class Americans, as well as lower and working-class Americans, are worried about declining real wages, job security, healthcare and the quality of education.[90] If public rhetoric and policy are aimed at these concerns of middle-class and working-class whites, as well as the needs of minorities, then a broader political coalition, which may be necessary to save public-sector affirmative action in some states, may be facilitated. Presently, many middle-class and working-class whites resent affirmative action, Aid to Families with Dependent Children (AFDC), public housing, Medicaid, and financial aid for college, mainly because they perceive that they pay for these programs, but do not benefit from them.[91] But the justification for race-neutral programs goes beyond saving public-sector affirmative action. Universal policies are compelled by the social rights of all individuals to a decent, livable material existence. When these rights are not the major priority of a government or a society, as they are not, currently, in the United States, then political divisions amongst groups with similar economic and quality-of-life interests is inevitable. As Amy Gutmann argues, where inadequate government responses to oppressive social and economic conditions exist, disadvantaged groups will be divided and fight over limited resources.[92] But, by arguing for the *common interests* of a majority of Americans, affirmative action defenders may facilitate their own goals and also promote a truly democratic society.

The argument for a comprehensive universal social welfare policy has other ramifications for affirmative action. Gutmann and Wilson both assert that affirmative action cannot reach the poorest Americans.[93] These groups, because they lack the economic and social resources to create healthy and secure environments in which they and their children can fully develop their natural talents, desperately need effective social welfare programs as a first step toward taking advantage of the government's equal opportunity initiatives. In the long run, moreover, universal programs have the potential to make affirmative action somewhat less controversial and less necessary. Sufficient economic and educational resources are likely, after several generations, to foster improved SAT scores and grades for the least favored Americans. Affirmative action may still be necessary in order to combat discrimination, but "merit" would be less of an issue if lower and working-class applicants' and minorities' test scores and grades were comparable to those of others.

THE NECESSITY OF "PUBLIC EDUCATION"

The argument for a universal social welfare policy and a race, class, and gender-based affirmative action cannot ignore such realities as working and middle-class resentment of minorities-fueled by belief in traditional concepts of merit, the ideology of individualism, and persistent racial stereotypes. All of these social phenomena contribute to white resentment of affirmative action and to their perception that the American government redistributes economic resources to the undeserving.

Working-class and middle-class whites, in the past two decades, have experienced great difficulty maintaining their economic status, yet alone achieving upward mobility, due to major structural shifts in the American economy. Between 1981 and 1991, 1.8 million manufacturing jobs disappeared in the United States, while the number of working-age Americans grew by 19.4 million.[94] In 1980, thirty-nine percent of Americans reported incomes between 20,000 and 50,000 dollars per year in real, constant dollars. But by 1989 this income group had decreased to thirty-five percent.[95] The cost of living has also escalated more dramatically than income, for many Americans, in the past three decades. A typical father in the 1950's or 1960s paid about fourteen percent of his monthly income for his housing costs. By the mid 1980's, that figure had climbed to forty-four percent.[96] Working-class Americans, moreover, experienced small income gains between 1980 and 1990, unlike previous generations that witnessed steady, significant gains in living standards.[97]

These economic pressures helped foster the perception that race-based affirmative action policies choose less qualified minorities over more qualified whites, and thus exacerbated white working and middle-class opposition to affirmative action. However, polls reveal that eighty-eight percent of whites do not believe they lost a job because of affirmative action. Even more surprising, ninety-eight percent do not believe they were rejected by a college because of affirmative action.[98] Since other polls reveal that few whites knew of others who had been hurt by race-based programs,[99] whites' anger toward these policies may express merely a form of displaced class anger at the collapse of the American economy. Whites are really angry at working hard, as did previous generations, yet being the first to experience growing economic and job insecurity. The belief, in short, that less qualified minorities are given preferences is rooted in traditional views of meritocracy, but is compounded by legitimate class anger. The need for public defenders of affirmative action to expand Americans' views of merit is essential, but so is their need to redirect public attention to class inequality.

The opposition to race-based affirmative action programs based on perceived merit violations is ironic, since legitimate class discontent and discrimination allowed lower-class and working-class whites to better their lives through patronage hiring and government contracting in previous decades. Jews, Poles, Irish, and Italians all advanced through this form of preferential hiring.[100] While civil service reforms attempted to hire and promote only by merit,[101] patronage still exists at almost all levels of government.[102] And past and present white beneficiaries of patronage do not oppose it. Working and middle-class whites who oppose affirmative action are, moreover, concerned with traditional qualifications and desert *only* in regards to race preferences— suggesting not only displaced class anger, but a racial content to affirmative action opposition. Persistent white adherence to stereotypes of blacks suggest that such whites still believe that blacks, in general, are less qualified than they are. Affirmative action appears to whites as an exploitative welfare program—giving blacks something they don't deserve, and denying those jobs and academic places to deserving whites. But high-profile defenders of affirmative action policy must unmask these stereotypes and dispel them by showing that many affirmative action beneficiaries in the private and public sector perform well. Proponents of a race, class, and gender-based affirmative action need to show that many disadvantaged students *of all races* perform somewhat lower than average, though disadvantaged minorities perform worse than disadvantaged whites because of their relative lack of educational and cultural resources. But many black affirmative action beneficiaries, defenders must show, have become successful professionals. Defenders must also expose traditional preferences for whites, thereby exposing in public debate our nation's double-standard of merit.

Other issues which are at the core of racial politics need to be addressed publicly in order to increase the chances for a stronger liberal coalition. Opposition to race preferences is, in part, rooted in the ideology of individualism. Black under-performance on traditional selection criteria appears to whites to be a result of the absence of a black work ethic. But again, affirmative action defenders must provide evidence demonstrating that blacks' economic, political, and social gains, in the last few decades, were not possible without persistent hard work. Affirmative action may provide opportunities, as does patronage, but making those chances work necessitates individual effort. Still, affirmative action's successes demonstrate that potential is not always identified by traditional methods.

Closely related to the belief in individual responsibility for one's plight is the narrow and destructive anti-structural individualist social analysis engaged in by most Americans. The wedge between working-class and middle-class white and black voters is encouraged by displaced class discontent, in part because Americans do not recognize structural barriers to economic success. Race becomes divisive because, as Barbara Ehrenreich points out, " . . . Americans are notorious for their lack of class consciousness or even class awareness. In the face of the most brutal personal dislocations, we lack a vocabulary to express our dismay".[103] The economic difficulties of the past two decades do not elicit anger at the economic structure or at upper-class Americans who continue to prosper, but facilitate resentment toward minorities, which results in white flight from the Democratic Party.[104] The American ethos of individualism precludes most Americans from detecting the structural nature of economic injustice. The popularity of Lockean individualist principles, which assert that a person's economic status is commensurate with one's effort renders other causes of economic difficulty imperceptible. Americans may recognize that increased global competition is partly responsible for job loss, but tend to blame government programs that assist groups who are perceived to reject the individualistic work ethic. This phenomenon results in mainstream attacks on means-tested social welfare programs, such as AFDC, food stamps, and affirmative action, which are perceived as redistributing economic opportunity to the undeserving. Populist anger has not yielded a populist cry for redistribution of wealth, increased wage equality, and effective government job programs. Thus, proponents of affirmative action must help redirect the focus of white resentment from racial to class injustice. Certainly, the advocacy of universal programs that address whites' job insecurity and other economic and quality of life concerns is integral to redirecting public anger. Defenders of affirmative action should also point out that, historically both whites and African-Americans have used nontraditional avenues to improve their economic power. Such a sense of commonality may help to facilitate a class-based politics. Exposing the traditional preferences of patronage, and the political and social networks used by white ethnic groups, which violate ordinal rankings of job candidates based on merit, may decrease whites' racial resentment by helping them to recognize the class roots of their economic anxieties. Whites blame affirmative action for violating merit but forget that "merit" is invoked only in popular resentment against race preferences. Defenders of affirmative action must also debunk irrelevant selection criteria, showing why the selection of African-Americans with lower test scores is not a violation of relevant qualification criteria.

Patronage and veterans' preferences are forms of affirmative action that have benefited white ethnic groups. However, obtaining jobs through these vehicles would not be considered fair by one who opposed affirmative action because they claim it violates traditional concepts of merit. When faced with the reality that many affirmative action opponents are the beneficiaries or the progeny of those who benefited from traditional preferences it is hard to maintain that affirmative action is unfair. Since merit was not such a divisive issue for traditional preferences, what is the difference i.e. why is it such a divisive issue for affirmative action? This question serves as a segue for a public debate about merit and fair, realistic selection criteria.

Yet exposing traditional preferences may not be sufficient to get whites to recognize their anxiety about job insecurity. Kahlenberg blames the left's failure to build a coalition advocating increased social spending for education, jobs, and health care on its fostering white obsession with race but not class. Middle-class liberal support of affirmative action for minorities that working class whites perceive as advantaged only increases whites' opposition to affirmative action.[105] However, Americans also need to understand class inequality. This requires that affirmative action defenders establish publicly the limits of American individualist ideology. Hard work, motivation, and perseverance cannot counter powerful structural forces, such as global competition and de-industrialization, which decrease the number of high-wage industrial jobs. Nor do children choose the class they are born into, and hardworking class-disadvantaged students may appear to have less academic potential then they may well have. Americans must be exposed to the realities of class stratification, which yields the generational reproduction of poverty and class position. Were class injustice exposed, white "Reagan Democrats" might abandon their obsession with race and "merit,"

and consider building a cross-racial political coalition demanding equal opportunity and increased economic power for the disadvantaged.

Working-class and lower-class whites might feel better about the Democratic Party if they, too, benefit from affirmative action. But race, merit, and
class issues must be publicly discussed and resolved. If this does not happen,
a cross-racial coalition may stand on purely instrumental motives, and race
and merit may again create intra-party dissent. Working and middle-class
whites may unite with racial minorities to form a progressive Democratic
Party *only* because of the public benefits they will receive. However, these
whites must make ideological changes. Such whites have to *believe* that traditional selection criteria can discriminate against African-Americans and the
class-disadvantaged. They must also recognize that strong individual effort
may *not* produce the good life for many Americans, and that racial stereotypes are intellectually wrong and socially destructive. If such changed attitudes do not occur in whites, their current beliefs about race, merit, and individualism may again become wedges as a response to economic discontent.
Affirmative action advocates need to engender public education and discussion about class realities, racism, merit, and competitive marketplace individualism if a progressive cross-racial political coalition is to have moral—
not just instrumental—underpinnings, and therefore be enduring.

A RACE, CLASS, AND GENDER-BASED
AFFIRMATIVE ACTION

Affirmative action needs to include poor and working-class white Americans. These groups suffer from disadvantages compared to middle-class
and upper-class whites, which impair their quest for material comfort. Due
to poorer education, less stable familial and neighborhood environments,
and fewer community resources, such as upwardly-mobile role models and
job information networks, disadvantaged whites, on average do not do as
well as others academically and economically. But as I have argued, the
potential to do well academically and professionally may be obscured
in disadvantaged persons. Colleges, employers, and government agencies
must seek to locate such potential ability by expanding their traditional
views of how potential is discerned. Affirmative action, which attempts to
broaden traditional selection criteria, can increase opportunities for lower
and working-class whites who have ability that has been obscured by their
backgrounds. Giving a plus to such individuals in hiring, higher education
admissions, and contract-awarding selection processes, will further the
goal of true equal opportunity.

Affirmative action for disadvantaged whites broadens government equal opportunity efforts, but must not replace such initiatives for middle-class African-Americans. Middle-income blacks are not free from racism and discrimination. They still face discrimination in hiring and promotion. These blacks also often live in racially segregated communities and go to segregated schools that isolate them from job networks, a better quality education, and pertinent knowledge about white mainstream culture. Middle-class African-Americans, on average, score lower on the SAT than do middle-class, working-class, and lower-class whites, and attain, on average, lower high school and undergraduate grades. But as I have argued, the lower traditional criteria for blacks results from inferior education and cultural differences, which must be combated by the public schools, starting at the elementary level and continuing through high school. Affirmative action attempts to decrease these disadvantages that middle-class blacks face. The increase in the African-American middle class over the past thirty years owes much to affirmative action.[106] The racism, discrimination, and traditional concepts of merit that persist into the 21st century make it implausible that such gains would have occurred under a color-blind policy. These successes also endorse the view that a broad conception of relevant qualifications is both morally compelling and achievable. Affirmative action defenders must also support the addition of disadvantaged whites as beneficiaries given the current political vulnerability of public sector affirmative action and the demand of social justice that such whites be given greater opportunities. Most major American corporations support affirmative action,[107] and a total roll-back of the policy by Congress in the near future seems unlikely.[108] But as shown in chapter one affirmative action remains vulnerable, especially at the state level. Adding class to race and gender-based policies may increase their popular support. Since most African-Americans work in the public sector, and because a college degree is often the gateway by which blacks enter the middle-class, affirmative action in the public sector and in college admissions needs stronger public support. However, as William Julius Wilson argues, public political rhetoric needs to be directed at the *common* economic and social concerns of both white and minority lower, working, and middle classes. These white groups have to be assured that liberal policies will address *their* socioeconomic needs and concerns. Race-neutral policies that provide greater opportunities for disadvantaged whites and that, simultaneously, decrease the economic anxiety of middle-class whites, may advance a progressive coalition that supports affirmative action. Adequate child-care, good schools, and a decent income are concerns of working *and* middle-class whites. These groups may be more supportive of affirmative action if they feel that they, too, benefit from social welfare policies that address their concerns. The addition of lower-class and working-class whites to affirmative action may also foster a new political force in American politics, and thereby make whites receptive to the benefits of universal programs. If these whites experience upward mobility as a result of such a race, class, and gender-based affirmative action program, they may support other liberal social welfare policy proposals. Whatever argument is made that attempts to eliminate the wedge in American racial politics, those who support progressive policies cannot ignore popular ideologies and entrenched beliefs. The rebuilding of a truly liberal Democratic Party stands a better chance if affirmative action defenders and progressives publicly challenge the racial double-standards about merit, and Americans' typical lack of class-consciousness. Such blinders comprise the ideological barriers that keep many white Americans from favoring affirmative action policies. But public information and dialogue about the limits of individualism, narrow notions of merit, and the real sources of white ethnics' upward mobility, may help re-focus white resentment from race to class. Such public education is crucial given that many whites who succumb to downward mobility hang on to these self-defeating and racial wedge-solidifying ideologies. Some Americans may be more receptive to liberal social welfare programs if they believe them to be morally imperative, instead of an impetus for higher taxes that they perceive will be redistributed to the undeserving.

Adding class considerations to affirmative action may provoke resentment in first-generation middle-class Americans. These Americans might believe that they are the rightful heirs of their parents' and grandparents' hard work and ambition. Affirmative action defenders can respond to such arguments by pointing out that many poor and working-class Americans' forbearers worked hard, but were underpaid. Defenders should also argue that some ambitious Americans from past generations were thwarted in realizing their goals by their personal circumstances and by the economic realities of a market economy. The law of supply and demand established the number of available high-wage jobs. In such an economy some of the ambitious and hard-working will not achieve their goal of the good life.

A race, class, and gender-based affirmative action has costs. It is inevitable that African-Americans, Hispanics, and women will face increased competition for academic places, jobs, promotions, and public contracts if class considerations are added to affirmative action. This reality makes the argument for a broadened view of selection criteria all the more imperative. The intensified competition that racial minorities would experience must not be exacerbated by traditional conceptions of merit that favor whites. Poor and working-class white beneficiaries must also be those who are truly disadvantaged. This does not mean that affirmative action should not consider poor children who went to good schools. However, selection decisions should involve many relevant criteria in order not to discriminate against a lower-class applicant who has lower traditional criteria and attended an inferior school. However, the potential of a multi-racial political coalition, which could occur, in part, by adding class considerations to affirmative action may well be worth the cost of increased competition. The American public desperately needs to see, for their own benefit, the power that class exercises in determining individual opportunity. By adding a class component to affirmative action, its defenders may begin to galvanize such a consciousness. To destroy the wedge of racial politics, whites must be made to see that the ideology of unlimited individual opportunity has its practical limits. Including disadvantaged whites in equal opportunity efforts could foster such new insights.

NOTES

1. Richard D. Kahlenberg, *The Remedy* (New York: Basic Books, 1996), pp. 83–101.

2. Harold Hodgkinson, "What Shall We Call People," in *Phi Delta Kappan*, October, 1995, pp. 176.

3. Kahlenberg, *The Remedy*, pp. 190–203.

4. Gary Pavela, "What's Wrong with Race-Based Affirmative Action?", in *Responding to the New Affirmative Action Climate*, Donald D. Gehring, ed. (San Francisco: Jossey–Bass Publishers, 1998), pp. 33–39.

5. Kahlenberg, *The Remedy*, p. 90.

6. Ibid., p. 94.

7. Ibid., p. 99.

8. Ibid., p. 129.

9. Ibid., p. 96.

10. Ibid., pp. 100–101.

11. James Crouse and Dale Trusheim, *The Case Against the SAT* (Chicago: Univesrity of Chicago Press, 1988), p. 163.

12. Stephen and Abigail Thernstrom, *America In Black and White* (New York: Simon and Schuster, 1997), p. 185.

13. William G. Bowen and Derek Bok, *The Shape of the River: Long Term Consequences of Considering Race in College and University Admissions* (Princeton, N.J.: Princeton University Press; 1998), p. 48.

14. Andrew Hacker, *Two Nations* (New York: Charles Scribner's Sons, 1992), p. 143.

15. *New York Times*, September 9, 1998, B10.

16. Hacker, *Two Nations*, p. 143.

17. *Philadelphia Inquirer*, April 25, 2004, C1.

18. Alan Wolfe, "The Affirmative Action Fact Gap" in *The New York Times Book Review*, October 25, 1998, pp. 15–16.

19. John A. Hartigan and Alexandra K. Wigdor, eds., *Fairness in Employment Testing* (Washington, D.C.: National Academy Press, 1989), Part 1, p. 42.

20. Jomills Henry Braddock II and James M. McPartland, "How Minorities Continue to be Excluded from Equal Employment Opportunities: Research on Labor Market and Institutional Barriers," *Journal of Social Issues*, Vol. 43, 1, (1987): pp. 12–19.

21. *Philadelphia Inquirer*, March 16, 1995. A1.

22. William Julius Wilson, *When Work Disappears*, pp. 198–199; Orlando Patterson, *The Ordeal of Integration* (Washington, D.C.: Counterpoint, 1997), pp. 161–167.

23. Douglas S. Massey and Nancy A. Denton, *American Apartheid: Segregation and the Making of the Underclass* (Cambridge, Mass.: Harvard University Press, 1993), p. 165.

24. Joleen Kirschenman and Kathryn M. Neckerman, "We'd Love to Hire Them, But …: The Meaning of Race for Employers," in *The Urban Underclass*, eds. Christopher Jencks and Paul E. Peterson (Washington, D.C.: Brookings Institution, 1991), pp. 223–231.

25. Hacker, *Two Nations*, p. 146. This is the central point of *Two Nations*.

26. *Philadelphia Inquirer*, October 20, 1994, A17.

27. 41 C.F.R., Part 60–2.23–2.24.

28. Orlando Patterson, *The Ordeal of Integration* (Washington, D.C.: Counterpoint, 1997), p. 10.

29. *Philadelphia Inquirer*, March 16, 1995, A9.

30. Ibid.

31. Ibid.

32. *Philadelphia Inquirer*, August 28, 2001, A14.

33. Bowen and Bok, *The Shape of the River*, p. 48.

34. *Philadelphia Inquirer*, October 9, 2003, A6.

35. Andrew Hacker, "Affirmative Action," *Dissent 212*, Fall 1995, pp. 466–468.

36. Bowen and Bok, *The Shape of the River*, p. 51.

37. Thomas Byrne Edsall and Mary D. Edsall, *Chain Reaction* (New York: W.W. Norton, 1992), chaps. 7–11.

38. Ibid., pp.153, 164, 225–226.

39. *New York Times*, November 5, 1998, B10.

40. Crouse and Trusheim, *The Case Against the SAT*, pp. 130–131.

41. Ibid., p. 163.

42. Susan Sturm and Lani Guinier, "The Future of Affirmative Action: Reclaiming The Innovative Ideal," *California Law Review*, Volume 84, 4, 1996, pp. 987–992.

43. Ibid., p. 991.

44. Ibid., pp. 990–991.

45. *Philadelphia Inquirer*, June 16, 2004, A1, A16.

46. Kahlenberg, *The Remedy*, pp. 93–94.

47. George R. LaNoue, "Split Visions: Minority Business Set-Asides," in *The ANNALS of The American Academy of Political Social Science*, Volume 523, eds., Harold Orlans and June O'Neill (Newbury Park: SAGE Publications, Inc., 1992), p. 110.

48. *Philadelphia Inquirer*, March 10, 1998, A18.

49. *Philadelphia Inquirer*, January 8, 1998, A3.

50. See Barbara R. Bergman, *In Defense of Affirmative Action* (New York: Basic Books, 1996), pp. 41–49, 156–160 and Samuel Cohn, *Race, Gender and Discrimination at Work* (Boulder, Colorado: Westview Press; 2000), pp. 14–27.

51. Sturm and Guinier, "The Future of Affirmative Action," p. 992.

52. Ibid., p. 993.

53. Ibid., p. 995.

54. *Philadelphia Inquirer*, March 16, 1995, A1.

55. Ibid.

56. Ibid.

57. Cohn, *Race, Gender, and Discrimination at Work*, pp. 15–16.

58. Ibid., pp. 17–18.

59. Ibid., pp. 15–17.

60. Barbara F. Reskin, "The Realities of Affirmative Action in Employment," in *Sex, Race and Merit*, eds. Faye Crosby and Cheryl Van De Veer (Ann Arbor, Michigan: The University of Michigan Press, 2000), p. 104.

61. Ibid., pp. 103–104.

62. Ibid., pp. 104–105.

63. Ibid., pp. 109.

64. Ibid., p. 110.

65. LaNoue, "Split Visions: Minority Business Set-Asides," p. 106.

66. Ibid.

67. Ibid., p. 110.

68. *Philadelphia Inquirer*, March 7, 1998, A2.

69. Ibid.

70. *Philadelphia Inquirer*, April 27, 1998, A1.

71. Gerald Torres and Penda D. Hair, "The Texas Test Case: Integrating America's Colleges," in *Chronicle of Higher Education*, October 4, 2000, B20.

72. Mary Frances Berry, "How Percentage Plans Keep Minority Students Out of College," in *Chronicle of Higher Education*, August 4, 2000, A48.

73. Torres and Hair, "The Texas Test Case," B20.

74. Catherine L. Horn and Stella M. Flores, *Percent Plans in College Admissions: A Comparative Analysis of Three States' Experiences* (Cambridge: The Civil Rights Project, 2002) Available at www.civilrightsproject.harvard.edu.

75. Patricia Marin and Edgar K. Lee, *Appearance and Reality in the Sunshine State: The Talented 20 Program in Florida.* (Cambridge: The Civil Rights Project, 2002) Available at www.civilrightsproject.harvard.edu.

76. Berry, "How Percentage Plans . . .," A48.

77. Ibid.

78. Torres and Hair, "The Texas Test Case," B20.

79. *Philadelphia Inquirer*, April 27, 1998, A1, A6.

80. Edsall and Edsall, *Chain Reaction*, p. 164.

81. Ibid., p. 153.

82. Ibid., pp. 225–226.

83. *The Gallup Poll* (Wilmington, Delaware: Scholarly Resources, Inc., 1996), p. 218.

84. *The Gallup Poll* (Wilmington, Delaware: Scholarly Resources, Inc., 1995), p. 43.

85. Jerome Karable, "Stuck in the Station," *The Nation*, Volume 265, December 15, 1997, p. 22.

86. *Philadelphia Inquirer*, November 1, 1996, A1.

87. *Philadelphia Inquirer*, May 30, 1995, F6.

88. Ibid.

89. William Julius Wilson, *When Work Disappears* (New York: Knopf, 1997), pp. 201–202.

90. Ibid., pp. 204–206.

91. Edsall and Edsall, *Chain Reaction*, chaps. 10–11.

92. K. Anthony Appiah and Amy Gutmann, *Color Conscious* (Princeton, New Jersey: Princeton University Press, 1996), pp. 148.

93. Appiah and Gutmann, *Color Conscious*, pp. 147–148 and William Julius Wilson, *The Truly Disadvantaged* (University of Chicago Press, 1987), p. 112.

94. Donald L. Barlett and James B. Steele, *America: What Went Wrong?* (Kansas City: Andrews and McMeel, 1992), p. xi.

95. Ibid., p. 4.

96. Barbara Ehrenreich, "Is The Middle Class Doomed?", in *The New York Times Magazine*, September 7, 1986, p. 50–51.

97. Edsall and Edsall. *Chain Reaction*, pp. 219–220, 196–197.

98. *The Gallup Poll* (Wilmington, Delaware: Scholarly Resources, Inc., 1995), p. 216.

99. Patterson, *The Ordeal of Integration*, pp. 148–152.

100. Edsall and Edsall, *Chain Reaction*, p. 254.

101. Jack C. Plano and Milton Greenberg, *The American Political Dictionary*, Ninth Edition (Fort Worth, Texas: Harcourt Brace College Publisher, 1990), pp. 218, 222.

102. Ibid., pp. 210–211, 218, 222.

103. Barbara Ehrenreich, "Is the Middle Class Doomed?", pp. 50–51.

104. Edsall and Edsall, *Chain Reaction*.

105. Richard D. Kahlenberg, "Class, Not Race", *The New Republic*, April 3, 1995, p. 24, 27.

106. Bowen and Bok, *The Shape of the River*.

107. See *The Wall Street Journal*, April 16, 1997, A17, and Alan Farnham, "Holding Firm On Affirmative Action", in Fortune, March 13, 1987, pp. 87–88.

108. *New York Times*, March 7, 1998, A9.

Chapter Four

Reapproachment: Moral, Pragmatic, and Political Implications

The central argument of this study, which has analyzed the political and intellectual history of affirmative action, suggests that the public defenders of the policy have not challenged Americans' reified concepts of merit. Yet they need to do so, now more than ever. The 1990's attacks on public sector affirmative action have resulted in its elimination in California and Washington. Affirmative action is most vulnerable when states vote on the policy through a referendum, and the re-election of George W. Bush has the potential of adding more conservative appointments to federal counts. The appeal of the anti-affirmative forces turns on their marshalling of public belief in traditional notions of qualifications, which assign inordinate significance to academic grades and employment and aptitude test scores, but exclude other relevant criteria. To turn back these forces, the political elites and public intellectuals who defend affirmative action need to propose and to demonstrate the argument presented here; that if solely traditional standards are used to determine who is "more qualified,' many racial minorities and economically disadvantaged college and job applicants will suffer discrimination. For these criteria do not always do what they claim to do, which is to measure long-run potential to perform well in college or at a job. Such a public defense of affirmative action is desperately needed because it adds a morally compelling content to its current justifications of "diversity" and "past discrimination." These latter defenses do not persuade many Americans because they do not critique or broaden the concept of merit. But defenders of affirmative action must also expand public discourse by offering alternative selection criteria for applicants. I have suggested that higher education, employment, and government institutions evaluate their candidates by looking at a broader range of relevant criteria.

John Skrentny has asked, albeit obliquely, why defenders of affirmative action have not argued that traditional preferences are unmeritocratic, according to traditional conceptions of merit, yet remain uncontroversial?[1] I argue
that the public proponents of affirmative action need to expose this double-
standard. White working-class and middle-class Americans should be con-
fronted with the "affirmative" political tactics that previous generations of
white ethnics were provided to advance economically. Such review may encourage these groups to reconsider the meanings of merit and desert. However, for such groups to support affirmative action, class needs to be added to
race and gender-based criteria. Not only blacks, but also Asians and whites of
lower and working-class background can also be victimized by narrow institutionalized beliefs about their qualifications. Those who defend affirmative
action need to argue that disadvantaged whites and Asians must be added to
the policy, while demonstrating that both race and class barriers to economic
mobility underscore the limitations of traditional selection criteria.

The broader conception of merit and desert has implications for the moral
defense of a race, class, and gender-based affirmative action policy. Such a
non-traditional approach to selection criteria also suggests new guidelines for
both the institutions, which implement, and those who enforce, affirmative
action. The purpose of this chapter is to discuss the moral, institutional and
political implications of the affirmative action defense argued in the previous
chapters.

MORAL IMPLICATIONS:
MULTIPLE RELEVANT SELECTION CRITERIA

This study demonstrates that affirmative action is controversial among both
the public and political elites because opponents perceive that it violates traditional conceptions of merit. The major critiques of affirmative action-
reverse discrimination, loss of self-respect to beneficiaries, and the need to
make affirmative action strictly class-based—pivot upon the concept of merit.
Those who argue that affirmative action discriminates against whites base this
view on their belief that less qualified minorities are admitted, hired, and promoted before more qualified whites. The theoretical underpinnings of the
self-respect critique also center around assumed merit violations; affirmative
action beneficiaries, who are aware that they may not have been the most
qualified, will lose self-respect. These critiques imply that qualified job and
higher education admission candidates can be objectively, and therefore
fairly, rank-ordered. As I suggest, this belief stems from American political
culture's narrow intellectual conception of individual effort and achievement,

which ignores structural barriers of not just gender and race, but also class discrimination. Americans have a strong attachment to the idea that individuals determine their quality of life, that individuals can overcome any obstacles by rational planning of day-to-day activity, and by consistently persevering toward long-term goals. As a result, many Americans are not sympathetic to the claim that some individuals and social groups are disadvantaged, and therefore compete for social goods on an unlevel playing field. Americans believe that the candidate with the highest test score has worked the hardest, and therefore *deserves* to be ranked first. Americans' rigid preferences for individual competition does not question the validity and rationality of the criteria used to evaluate candidates. Many Americans are convinced of the power of the individual will to erase the barriers to achievement posed by inequality and so dismiss critical analysis of the criteria and methods used for determining competence.

Unlike the claims of reverse discrimination and loss of self-respect, the class critique of affirmative action implicitly debunks traditional merit concepts. Richard Kahlenberg, a major proponent of class-based affirmative action, argues that lower class and working class individuals who have done "fairly well," but are not the "most qualified," according to traditional standards, should be given preference in jobs, college admissions, and public contracts. Kahlenberg implies that traditional standards *miss* some qualified people. But he does not make this a central argument. Kahlenberg subordinates questionable standards of merit to his major justification for class-based policy, which is class-disadvantage. In so doing, he ignores their adverse impact on middle-class blacks, which will occur if tests and grades are used as the sole selection criteria. Although Kahlenberg implicitly acknowledges the adverse impact of these criteria on the poor and working classes of all races, his emphasis on class disadvantage as the sole or pivotal cause of barriers to economic mobility misses the opportunity to provoke a public debate on merit. Kahlenberg thus fails to argue for multiple relevant selection criteria, other than adding class disadvantage, but he does advocate eliminating race as one qualification among many.

The public figures that defend affirmative action rarely criticize American political culture. The implied charge by Kahlenberg that hard-working, self-motivated, and strong-willed individuals are thwarted by "neutral" and freely-chosen institutional practices, which profess to ensure equal treatment of candidates, contradicts core American beliefs. However, this omission in public affirmative action debate obscures the *moral* need for a race, class, and gender-based policy. Affirmative action regulations recognize that if traditional selection criteria ad methods of recruitment are used exclusively, many fewer African-Americans will be admitted to colleges, hired or promoted, or awarded public contracts. There will also be fewer women in upper-level managerial jobs, and fewer female-owned firms will be awarded public contracts.[2] If affirmative action is not extended to disadvantaged whites and Asians, they too will continue to be victims of traditional criteria. The public defense of affirmative action often justifies it as a policy that helps to diversify institutions and thus redresses past discrimination. But such defenses sound hollow to many because they are not linked to broader conceptions of merit. Public supporters of affirmative action have ignored the implications of the 1971 *Griggs* decision. The Griggs opinion argued that traditional selection criteria could be discriminatory if they did not successfully identify relevant job-specific qualifications. It is imperative that more institutions rethink their recruitment and selection practices,[3] and that the government agencies which enforce affirmative action mandate that institutional selection criteria be job and task-related.[4] I have shown that many affirmative action beneficiaries have succeeded, and that institutions which use such fair and relevant standards have not abandoned legitimate qualifications.[5] Absent affirmative action, universities will be less likely to lower test scores and grade bars for black applicants, and the life opportunities of truly qualified minorities and disadvantaged whites will be dramatically harmed.[6]

The moral imperative for race, class, and gender-based affirmative action is also compelled by the persistence of racial, class, and gender prejudice and discrimination. Again, Americans' faith in competitive individualism is implicated. This faith in individual meritocracy retards analysis of social phenomena by rendering invisible the underlying causes of social ills. Those who believe that strong applications of individual will are the key to success do not perceive racial barriers when overt discrimination, such as Jim Crow signs, have disappeared. But as shown in chapter 2 and 3 less overt institutional racial discrimination persists, as do gender prejudices. Therefore, affirmative action, which attempts to make institutional actors cognizant of negative stereotyping, is doubly necessary. The immorality of present discrimination—be it racist or sexist, both reinforced by limiting concepts of merit is attacked by affirmative action.

The Griggs Business Necessity Test

The affirmative action defense needs to make use of the Griggs' business necessity test. This principle attempts to protect those who apply for jobs and higher education admissions by requiring that any selection criteria be relevant to the abilities needed for the required job. Since institutional practices are checked by the business necessity requirement, the applicants with lower traditional qualifications have legal recourse if they believe that firms or colleges rejected them unfairly. Affirmative action defenders must argue that the business necessity principle should be a guideline for determining if the chosen criteria are fair. The business necessity principle gets communities and institutions to start thinking about relevant job and academic admissions criteria. Selection committees will interpret the meaning of "business necessity" according to their particular economic, social, or political needs. But absent such a principle, the likelihood of selection officials or committees intentionally or unintentionally choosing discriminatory criteria is greater than if business necessity is used as a guideline. Americans' long- term belief in the objectivity of tests, grades, and academic degrees as the sole selection criteria renders the disadvantaged vulnerable to such biases.

Diversity and Moral Implications

Many political elites who defend affirmative action have justified it on the grounds that it increases racial diversity. However, they do not present 'diversity' as a moral argument. As explained in *Bakke*, diversity is a college admissions strategy for broadening students' intellectual and cultural experiences. Current political elite defenses use the *Bakke* argument, but do not link diversity with a critique of merit. These defenders can tie the case for diversity to moral considerations if they show that narrow and unfair selection criteria necessitate affirmative action, and creates a need for diversity goals. If fair and relevant standards are used, diversity is increased; colleges and university have admitted and graduated many African- Americans who would not have been admitted under traditional standards. Diversity is further strengthened if public affirmative action defenders argue and demonstrate that present racial discrimination, also, thwarts diversity; if discrimination did not persist, then diversity programs would not be necessary. Affirmative action defenders must show that diversity intends to decrease present racial discrimination, and is not just a policy which attempts to expand the variety of perspectives within institutions.

POLICY IMPLICATIONS: INSTITUTIONALIZING FAIR NOTIONS OF MERIT

Institutions which adhere to traditional concepts of merit must reevaluate their conceptions of legitimate and necessary qualifications, and government agencies which oversee diversity efforts enforce such broader views. This requires not only that qualifications be valid, but also that traditional concepts of merit be expanded. A good-faith effort should be made to reevaluate selection criteria according to the view of qualifications suggested by this study. Currently, some institutions do not make tests, grades, or degrees controlling factors when selecting applicants. SAT critic David Owen finds that colleges and universities often do not reject applicants solely because of low SAT scores, but also look at other qualifications,[7] such as grades and references. Some colleges will lower SAT and GPA bars for racial minorities, and other groups. When one considers that African Americans tend to underperform on tests, and that Blacks have gained more middle-class jobs since the 1960's, it is evident that some employers do not view tests as definitive hiring criteria. However, a survey conducted by Jomills Henry Braddock III and James McPartland reveals that tests, grades and degrees are still important qualifications in hiring and promotion.[8] These traditional criteria are appropriate if they are valid, but so are other relevant qualifications. However, institutions must also rethink the assumption that qualified competitors for academic places and jobs can be objectively ranked in strict order. Affirmative action has encouraged employers and colleges to put less weight on traditional qualifications, especially tests and grades. But a new perspective, which debunks strict ordinal ranking, and expands narrow views of legitimate criteria, may lend a sounder moral and logical justification to affirmative action.

This study suggests that the government agencies which enforce affirmative action need to conduct compliance reviews that are informed by, and also encourage, a broader view of merit. When agencies such as the OFFC and the Department of Education evaluate the diversity plans and efforts of businesses and colleges, the selection criteria these institutions use must be scrutinized. Affirmative action efforts will be stronger if enforcement involves these changes. If tests which cause disparate impact when significant percentages of racial groups fail, are challenged only by employees and applicants, diversity efforts are slowed and some tests and /or other criteria will not be challenged. But if enforcement agencies evaluate selection and promotion criteria, and not just racial, class and gender statistics and outreach efforts, institutions will get the message that their standards must be both valid *and* broad. A "good-faith effort" to diversify workforces will, therefore, *require* validation and expansion of selection criteria. This is especially pertinent when one considers a survey of 202 CEO's of Fortune 500 and Service 500 corporations, which revealed that only 42 percent believed that they had made a genuine affirmative action effort. A major difficulty in achieving diversity, according to these companies, is too few "qualified" minorities.[9] If the notions of what "qualified" means are determined by looking at a wide range of criteria, then corporate equal-opportunity efforts may be more fruitful. If, as one example, the Glass Ceiling Commission's finding that advanced academic degrees are requirements for corporate upward mobility is scrutinized for validity, a broader range of legitimate criteria may be suggested. Such a new perspective may increase the number of minorities who are perceived by corporations to be *truly* qualified.

Employment

For many jobs, minimal essential qualifications can be established. This may facilitate larger pools of qualified candidates, who are racial minorities, women, and economically disadvantaged, than afforded when institutions use only traditional methods. The concept of business necessity can be used to establish essential qualifications. In *United States vs Paradise* (1987) the Supreme Court said: "Of the 60 Blacks who took the [Alabama Department of Public Safety's Promotion] test, only 5(8.3%) were listed in the top half of the promotion register; the highest ranked black candidate was number 80 [out of 262 applicants]."[10] These invalidated promotion procedures were used since 1972 despite numerous federal court orders to institute fair procedures.[11] As *Paradise* implies a test that disqualifies nearly every black applicant is suspect and must be interrogated.

Griggs requires that employers' selection procedures accurately predict job performance. A qualification must be a "business necessity". This means that a hiring criterion must bear a significant relationship to the successful performance of the job for which it is required. For example, requiring that teachers, at any education level be fairly articulate is a business necessity. If college degrees are required for a job, then the knowledge gained from a specific degree must be *necessary* for performing that job. Griggs upheld the meaning of "validity" as explicated in EEOC's Guidelines on Employment Testing Procedures. The Guidelines required that employers have ". . . data demonstrating that the test is predictive or significantly correlated with important elements of work behavior which . . . are relevant to the job . . . for which candidates are being evaluated."[12]

Post-Griggs cases demonstrated that the Supreme Court reads "business necessity" and "job related" rationally, broadly, and judiciously, case by case, therefore suggesting a guideline for employers to establish fair selection criteria. In *Albemarle Paper Company vs Moody* (1975), the Court found that the plaintiff had not validated two general ability tests used for employment and promotion. Specifically, " The [validation] study . . . involved no analysis of the attributes of, or the particular skills needed in, the studied job groups," and involved vague subjective criteria which left ". . . no way to determine whether the criteria . . . were sufficiently related to the Company's legitimate interest in job-specific ability to justify a testing system with a racially discriminatory impact."[13] Both *Griggs* and *Albemarle* require that selection methods be rational-able to distinguish the qualified from the unqualified and marginally qualified. Neither decision precludes using *appropriate* selection methods, but articulates the government's concern that these be fair, and tries to foster this concern in employers. *Albemarle* and *Griggs* foster concern for selection fairness; why should selection be based on *assumed* validity? *Griggs* implies that employers must not choose tests or other hiring criteria arbitrarily. To do so is to presume too casually the criteria's relevant relationship to the particular job(s) for which it is required. Affirmative action critics claim that validation assaults employers' freedom, but *assumed* validity equally compromises fair hiring practices.

The broadly constructed meanings of "business necessity" and "job related" bear witness in *Washington vs Davis* (1977); and *New York City Transit Authority vs Beazer* (1979). In *Washington vs Davis*, a police department's written personnel test (test 21), which had a disparate impact on black applicants, was found to be job-related. The Court argued that ". . . some minimum verbal and communicative skill would be very useful, if not essential to satisfactory progress in the training regimen."[14] Test 21 was found to bear a significant relationship to recruitee success in the police training program in a validation study.[15] As in *Albemarle*, the court interprets job-relatedness case by case, but the validation study accurately predicted the performance of recruitees in the training program-unlike the Albemarle validation study, which did not. The tests at issue in Griggs[16] have no relationship to the jobs for which they are used, but police officers do need to have good oral and written communication skills. The police recruitment test, moreover, was passed by many blacks; 44 percent of the new recruits were black. Though more blacks failed the test than whites, many blacks passed. A more suspect test had been used by the Alabama Department of Public Safety; few blacks passed, and the test had not been validated. Disparate impact on its face, in *Washington vs Davis*, requires a validation of the rationality of the selection methods that produced it. Subsequent cases further the broad and rational construction of *Griggs* principles.

The Court ruled, in *Dothard vs Rawlinson*, that height and weight requirements bear no relationship to strength, and therefore are not job-related for prison guards. Alabama corrections officials failed to show that the requirement was job-related; corrections officials ". . . produced no evidence correlating the height and weight requirements with the requisite amount of strength thought essential to good job performance."[17] However, maintaining a case-by-case treatment of disparate impact, the Court found that gender was job-related because "The likelihood that inmates would assault a woman because she was a woman would pose a real threat not only to the victim . . . but also to the basic control of the penitentiary . . ."[18] The Court cited evidence that twenty percent of male prisoners in the Alabama penitentiaries are sex offenders, and maintained that male is ". . . a bona fide occupational qualification for . . . [a] correctional counselor in a "contact" position in an Alabama male maximum-security penitentiary."[19] It is rational to assume that female correctional counselors are at substantial risk in contact positions in Alabama prisons. However, no evidence exists that height and weight are, in this context, job-related.

In *New York Transit Authority vs Beazer, the* Transit Authority's narcotics rule, which postponed employment eligibility for methadone patients, was upheld as "job-related." Former Transit Authority employees and applicants claimed the rule had a disparate impact. The Court found that the statistical showing of disparate impact was weak, but that, even if valid, the narcotics rule was rational and job-related since methadone patients are still in treatment, and therefore have not established a drug-free life. The Court ruled that ". . . as long as a treatment program . . . continues, a degree of uncertainty persists."[20] Beazer supports that job-relatedness is broadly construed and applied case by case.

The cases just discussed demonstrated how employers can implement Griggs principles as a way to establish relevant qualifications for specific jobs. Once necessary criteria are established other non-essential criteria can be considered as part of the whole mix of qualifications. Diversity criteria, race, class and gender, and other non-essential plus factors add to the total qualification profile of specific jobs. For example, if a selection decision comes down to 2 applicants, both of whom possess the essential skills and other relevant non-skill criteria, employers can then look at the non-essential pluses that each candidate brings to the job. A diversity plus or pluses of one candidate can be weighted against other factors, e.g. the computer expertise of the other applicant which is not essential for the specific job, but could be helpful to less computer experienced co-workers. Selection committees would have to consider their business's or institution's most pressing needs, diversity may be one, to make the final decision.

Higher Education

An 'academic necessity' guideline for college selection, similar to that of business necessity for employers is not as applicable. For jobs, essential qualifications can often be established, and the absence of one such criteria could drop an applicant from consideration. However, in college admissions the essential qualification is academic potential, the absence of which is not discernible by looking at any one factor in the mix of selection criteria. To

illustrate we can consider the following hypothetical cases. A college applicant with only average high school grades, but good references and an impressive interview, where motivation and intelligence were demonstrated,
should be considered for admission. Similarly an applicant with good high
school grades and references, but lower SAT scores should not be disqualified
from consideration. No one negative factor, SAT or GPA should be controlling. Other non-academic criteria, e.g. diversity, extra-curricular activities,
and, or hardship should also be parts of the applicant's profile, and weighted
according to the institutional objectives at the present time. Academic potential is not discernible or rendered non-existent by looking at one criteria, unlike in some jobs where a single requirement may be crucial to the successful
performance of that job.

   Diversity is often an institutional objective, for higher education and employers, at present. Diversity is also a societal goal, even the conservative
U.S. president George W. Bush has diversified his cabinet, but how much
weight does this accord to diversity as one of many non-academic and non-
job skill qualifications? Race, gender and class would be a strong plus in an
applicant profile because of their many positives; fostering good race rela-
tions, broadening individual experience, breaking down stereotypes, and at-
tracting untapped clienteles. Of course, an institution may have a crucial
need for a qualification other than diversity at a particular time, and this criteria would be very strong at that time.

Public Contracts

The business necessity guide can apply to the awarding of public contracts
to businesses. The essential qualification regarding contracts is effective
job performance. Government agencies can discern if a business is qualified by looking at a company's track record through references, and its
knowledge of the specifics needed to accomplish the present job. New
businesses should be interviewed to get a sense of their initial set-up,
amount of capital, quality of staff and their previous work experience, to
discern if they are a good risk. Non-essential qualifications can then be
considered. The location of a business is an important criteria if the community that it serves is economically depressed, and, or doesn't have many
similar ventures—if the business is successful others may pop up. The social goals of diversity and decreasing stereotypes would make gender and
race important selection criteria; female plumbers and carpenters and
African-American entrepreneurs in non-black areas both illustrate the
broader social import of diversity.

WEIGHTING DIVERSITY CRITERIA

A race, class, and gender-based affirmative action policy that gives a plus for each of these factors favors an applicant who possesses two or all three of the qualifications. A qualified lower-class black woman would, theoretically, be most favored. However, other considerations such as institutional and societal context, and the relevant technical skills required to perform a particular job, need to be weighed. A school district or a specific school may have never had a black male science teacher from a lower-class family, while it does currently employ two black female physical education teachers. In determining who will be selected as the science teacher, among applicants which include qualified black and white males and females from lower-class and working-class backgrounds, said school district has to consider several factors. While it already employs two black teachers, they are both female. A black female physical education teacher, moreover, is not as powerful a weapon by which to attack negative stereotypes about black intelligence as is a black science teacher. Although, the former would be quite valuable if she was the boys' gym teacher or coach. In this school, a qualified black male science teacher may be *most* valuable to achieving diversity goals. But such a school district may also have to consider its representation of white teachers who come from lower or working-class backgrounds. The decision-makers should always be guided by the question. "What candidate would be most valuable to the achievement of our institutional goals at this time?"

The following scenario further illustrates the difficulties that institutions may encounter regarding which diversity criteria is more relevant in a specific context. A white job candidate from a lower or working class background may have a higher score on a valid test, than a middle-class African-American candidate. Class mobility and racial progress are both at issue here. Both social goals are important, but which is more important would have to be determined by institutional context i.e. institutions would have to determine how much progress they have made with both goals to support which criteria is most relevant.

College selection committees need to consider that lower and working-class whites have, on average, higher SAT scores than lower, working-class, and middle-class African-Americans.[21] Some of the SAT differential is attributable to white students who benefit from going to middle-class and suburban schools, but become "poor" through divorce.[22] Colleges and universities can check both parents' educational background and income to ensure that only the *truly disadvantaged* are helped. But among disadvantaged applicants, traditional selection criteria cannot be the deciding factor in admissions. They need to comprise only one portion of that criteria. In itself, the inclusion of disadvantaged whites and Asians in affirmative action in higher education admission dramatically increases the competition for places.[23] Exacerbating this competition is the fact that working-class Asians also have higher average SAT scores than do lower-class and working-class blacks, as well as higher SAT scores than those of the average middle-class African-American.[24] Therefore, colleges could lessen the increased competition for scare places for blacks, once class begins to count in affirmative action, by evaluating applicants according to many criteria, that place only the truly disadvantaged whites and Asians in affirmative action pools. This is not to suggest that poor Asians who have higher SAT scores and grades than poor blacks should not be considered disadvantaged, as wealthy Asians score, on average, at least 208 points higher than do poor Asians.[25] However, SAT scores and grades should not solely determine selection among the disadvantaged.

GOALS

How should diversity be implemented? Hiring, admission, and contract-awarding goals are necessary because they increase institutions' awareness of their selection patterns. As this study shows, American institutions and society are by no means free of racial and gender prejudices and discrimination. A majority of corporations admit to putting forth weak affirmative action efforts; but abandoning goals would weaken such efforts even further. Such companies would have even less motivation to make solid efforts. But this does not mean that affirmative action seeks, or should seek, proportional representation. Requiring that African-Americans must equal their percent of the national or local population, in each and every job category, would be unrealistic. Racial and ethnic groups do not choose careers in the same numbers as their proportion of a population. Such a mandate would encourage institutions to hire and promote unqualified people.

What, then, should goals be based upon? Goals must reflect the context of an institution, but also consider the number of minorities, women, and class-disadvantaged persons who are potentially qualified for specific jobs in the local areas. A school district's teachers may be two percent back, but the number of qualified unemployed black teachers, in the locale may be large, and thus capable of increasing the low percentage of black teachers. Increasing the percentage of black teachers, in this case, may be attainable, but in local areas, which have a dearth of qualified Black teachers, it would be difficult. However, African-American teachers or trainees from outside the locale can be recruited with financial incentives. But the goal serves to motivate the school district to ensure that its students and employees do not experience a homogeneous environment. Attaining a goal of ten percent black teachers is less important than frequent social and intellectual exchange with minorities. This can only be experienced by white students and employees if a school has a reasonable amount of minority teachers and administrators. School districts should assess their level of integration. A "reasonable amount" should be determined through democratic debate in institutions, but such determinations will vary according to the differing realities of local areas. Businesses, which have many African-Americans, women, or workers from disadvantaged background in lower-level jobs, but few in upper-level positions, need to scrutinize their practices. This doesn't require that they have ten percent African-Americans as senior-level managers, but it does mean that they establish a realistic goal and make sincere efforts to attain it. If the selection criteria for such jobs are proper and candidate pools are diverse, these goals will be achievable. If institutions make genuine efforts to diversify, then racial, gender, and class workforce statistics will take care of themselves or be moot. Businesses that have *realistic* numbers of minorities in all positions are diverse; a company that has two percent Black senior managers may be as diverse as can be expected at present, given its local and institutional context. The Glass Ceiling Commission estimates that it takes an average of twenty-five years to become a corporate senior-level manager.[26] Although a broader conception of who is qualified may reduce this length of time, the success of diversity efforts depends on choosing the qualified. In some institutions, jobs, and locales, the availability of candidates who are minority, female, or from disadvantaged backgrounds, may be low. In other contexts, a higher ratio of female and minority lower-level managers may indicate that more of a vigorous affirmative action effort is needed. Institutions must be prime movers of social progress; the libertarian notion of a private realm, insulated by market necessities from social responsibilities, cannot foster diversity.

Affirmative action admissions goals for higher education are important since college degrees remain the gateway to enter many professions. The larger the number of African-Americans, women, and class-disadvantaged persons who perform a variety of professional jobs, the greater is the attack on stereotypes. Fair selection criteria, which use a broad-based assessment of academic potentiality, can counter the adverse impact of disadvantaged backgrounds and facilitate diversity. As with hiring and promotion, admissions goals have to be realistically attainable, and non-achievement of goals must not be automatically regarded as weak efforts or discriminatory, as long as colleges and universities make rigorous efforts.

Goals for the allocation of public contracts should also be established according to the availability of qualified female, minority or low-income business in a local population, and reasonable results should be attained if public agencies make strong diversity efforts.

The Army's attempts to diversify its upper ranks illustrates the successful use of rational criteria and approach to goals. Unmet goals are reviewed, but further attempts to promote minorities are not made if qualified candidates cannot be found. Significantly, candidates are evaluated for relevant past assignments, performance ratings, and training, in *addition* to education level and physical standards.[27] This broad notion of qualifications enables the Army to select from a racially diverse pool. Therefore, the preference for a minority is for one who is as qualified as any other strong candidate. Supporting these diversity efforts is the Army's close monitoring of its officers' treatment of minorities and dedication to diversity; officers are evaluated according to their commitment to equal opportunity.[28]

LONGEVITY

A federal judge, recently, ordered the Boston Police Department to end its affirmative action hiring plan on the grounds that its goals had been met.[29] Institutions should be realistic, i.e. if a hiring, admission, or awarding goal is reached, affirmative action efforts can be relaxed. The amount of progress made indicated the amount of attention and effort needed regarding diversity. However, oversight is always necessary, institutions and government agencies must remain abreast of the status of diversity in hiring, contracts, and college admissions, even if substantial progress has been achieved. The persistence of racism and discrimination, conservative trends in Americans politics, and human nature, the human tendency to fall back on old, limiting practices, require such vigilance.

POLITICAL IMPLICATIONS: FROM RACIAL RESENTMENT TO A COMMON CLASS STRUGGLE

I have argued that diversity and anti-discrimination efforts on behalf of African-Americans will be dramatically weakened if affirmative action is rolled back, eliminated, or rendered solely class-based. This claim needs to be the major focus of political defenders of affirmative action. Defenders of affirmative action must aggressively seek to broaden support for the policy by challenging entrenched views of merit and desert and by arguing for the addition of disadvantaged whites as beneficiaries. Affirmative action defenders should support a race, class, and gender-based policy. As

Kahlenberg shows, economic disadvantages may unfairly impede the opportunities of lower and working-class persons of all races. Political defenders of affirmative action can use this opportunity to talk about class to buttress public support for affirmative action. White resentment of race preferences is tied up with displaced class anger, as well as the belief that traditional notions of merit are valid. Former President Bill Clinton alluded to such when he stated in a 1995 speech, ". . . [affirmative action] did not cause the great economic problems of the American middle class."[30] However, Clinton and other public defenders of affirmative action need to take this argument further. Global competition and corporate down-sizing have recently restricted the job security and social mobility of working-class and middle-class whites. Absent from American public discourse is a tradition of class analysis that would explain the current economic struggles as emanating from domestic and global economic shrifts, and not from affirmative action. Affirmative action defenders need to demonstrate that economic anxiety about real wage decreases and job loss is a legitimate expression of class-based anger. Such an argument would hope to redirect whites' resentment of alleged racial injustice against whites to resentment of economic injustice to all disadvantaged Americans. Affirmative action defenders may best redirect public debate by challenging the limitations of the ethic of competitive individualism. The necessity for many American families to have two adult wage-earners[31] attests to such limitations; these families are working hard, but do not enjoy the economic gains that such effort generated for their parents and grandparents.

The political defense of affirmative action, by focusing on past and present class, race, and gender discontent, must forge a new understanding of merit. White ethnic immigrant groups in America were motivated by their disadvantaged class position to obtain patronage jobs and public contracts. Ethnic discrimination had resulted in, or perpetuated, economic inequalities among whites. White ethnics overcame these barriers by using their electoral power.[32] These groups did not object to how they were selected for jobs. Even now, for example, when Italian-owned construction companies subcontract with other Italian-owned businesses, few citizens protest that the latter may not be the most qualified. Other traditional preferences, such as veterans', athletes', academic legacies, and job networks, which have benefited whites for decades are not denounced as violations of just merit and desert. Political defenders of affirmative action must point this out in order to encourage a public analysis of merit and to decrease racial resentment.

Indeed, the survival of traditional preferences demonstrates that many whites come to revere "merit" only in response to affirmative action. This is not to claim that all selection criteria and conceptions of desert are pragmatically useless or intellectually baseless, but it does provoke a question for public debate: What do we mean by just merit and desert?

The double standard regarding merit suggests that racial stereotypes play a role in public opposition to affirmative action. If significant percentages of Irish or Jewish Americans would do poorly on a standardized test(s), the qualifications of these groups would not likely be the focus of public controversy. Such a phenomenon is rooted in the persistence of racial prejudice; black under-performance on tests reinforces the perception that many African-Americans lack a strong motivation to succeed. While the need to challenge traditional concepts of merit and desert is the major gap in the public defense of affirmative action, entrenched racial stereotypes interact with these concepts, exposing an intellectual terrain that defenders need to explore publicly.

If the affirmative action defense advocates a strong universal social welfare policy, it may further refocus popular resentment from race to class. Currently, affirmative action is symbolic to many whites of a social welfare system that they believe unfairly redistributes social goods from deserving white working class taxpayers to the "undeserving" minority poor. But if federal programs, such as affordable child-care, an increased minimum wage, and the addition of class to affirmative action, were implemented, the economic struggles of working and middle-income whites would be less burdensome, and their resentment of African-Americans less vitriolic.

The self-respect critique of affirmative action has been much less salient for the American public than the belief that "merit violations" cause reverse discrimination. However, by responding to the claim that the policy damages African-Americans' self-confidence, affirmative action proponents can elevate the debate. Impressive increases in the black middle- class over the last thirty years suggest that the policy does not damage blacks' self-regard. The opportunities created by affirmative action have given African-Americans the chance to show their ability to succeed. The claim that black beneficiaries of affirmative action lose self-respect is based on the assumption that they are unqualified, or less qualified, than others with whom they compete. But if defenders point out the studies, discussed in chapter two, of affirmative action beneficiaries that demonstrate how many have performed well, and also highlight the economic gains of blacks, then the weaknesses of traditional concepts of merit become clear. This study also shows that the long-term perceptual distortions about affirmative action must be countered in order to increase support for the policy. Qualifications have not been rendered obsolete or meaningless by affirmative action, nor by the *Griggs* decision. Indeed, studies of affirmative action hiring programs find little proof to substantiate the claims of qualification abandonment. The perception that affirmative action lowers or dismisses valid selection criteria revolves around highly-publicized cases and political battles such as *Gratz v. Bollinger, Bakke, Hopwood,* and the California Civil Rights Initiative. These expose the fact that affirmative action programs often lower traditional admissions hurdles. Opponents of such policies assume that fair and objective qualifications are being ignored, and point to high minority college dropout rates as evidence for their claims. However, political and public defenders of these programs need to argue that many African-Americans face economic, educational and cultural barriers that middle-class whites do not.[33] Defenders must also show that the percentages of blacks with academic degrees have risen dramatically since colleges have instituted affirmative action.[34] Since some affirmative action beneficiaries are graduating, the objectivity of traditional criteria must be re-evaluated. Indeed, the high dropout rate of whites suggests that a universal problem exists. Many college students of all races are underprepared for success in higher education.[35] Both affirmative action and traditional higher education selection process are imperfect, but the former has provided many truly qualified African-Americans with opportunities. Affirmative action has opened doors for these blacks to make significant social and professional contributions to American society. Yet, the traditional admissions process would have rejected these *qualified* minorities.

The belief that affirmative action has caused valid qualifications to become irrelevant is debunked further by the post-*Griggs* Supreme Court cases.[36] As shown in this chapter, these cases, clarify the meaning of *Griggs'* requirement of 'business necessity' and 'job-related' qualifications. In their decision, the Supreme Court found some criteria and tests to be valid, but others to be irrelevant at predicting performance on specific jobs. Clearly, the Court has not waged a "war on testing," nor left the free market vulnerable to government regulations which put proportional representation of women and minorities before efficiency considerations. The post-Griggs cases do not automatically equate disproportionate racial workplace statistics or test results with discrimination; but they do analyze the criteria which produced them to discern if they are job-related. Affirmative action defenders need to show, using these cases and the studies of affirmative action beneficiaries, that the policy has not abandoned *legitimate* selection criteria.

The perception that race preferences have caused widespread discrimination against whites[37] is contradicted by public opinion polls. Gallup surveys from 1995 found that eighty-eight percent of whites believe that they have never been denied a job due to affirmative action. This survey also revealed that ninety-two percent of whites do not believe that affirmative action had ever cost them a promotion, and ninety-eight percent do not think that they had lost a school admission because of the policy.[38]Harris polls conducted in 1995 found similarly small percentages of whites who knew of others who had been hurt by affirmative action.[39] Public proponents of affirmative action can use these findings to argue that whites do not reveal widespread personal experience of alleged "reverse discrimination." However, debunking this persistent distortion goes beyond merely pointing to these surveys. Despite whites' largely benign experience of racial preferences, enough negative perception of affirmative action exists to fuel electoral battles and result in hurtful roll-backs of the policy, such as California's Proposition 209 and Washington's Proposition 200. Redressing the perception of widespread white injury involves a critical analysis of merit and desert that may derail opposition to affirmative action and thus avoid future electoral battles. A compelling argument for a rational position on selection criteria can decrease the influence that the wording of proposition 209 had on its victory. Proposition 209 asked California voters if they favored banning race as a criterion for *discrimination* or *preferential treatment* in the public sector.[40] Certainly, the American theoretical predilection for liberal equality of opportunity influenced a majority to favor such a ban. But a broader conception of fair treatment, influenced by a rational, realistic concept of "merit," may have helped to defeat Propositions 209 and 200. The argument must be made publicly that qualified job, admissions, and contract candidates often cannot be objectively rank-ordered, and that the pool of the qualified may include some applicants who are judged to be so despite possessing somewhat lower traditional criteria. Such public arguments may give pause to those who would use such hotbutton terms as "reverse discrimination" and "preferential treatment," decreasing the efficacy of such language for anti-affirmative action forces.

Support for affirmative action may increase if high-profile defenders attack the perception that hiring goals actually function as rigid quotas. If affirmative action policy required inflexible quotas, seventy-five percent of the government contractors reviewed in 1994–95 would not be non-compliant, according to the Office of Federal Contract Compliance (OFCCP).[41] Rigid, inflexible quotas would *mandate* that specific percentages of blacks be hired, or promoted, to various jobs within a short-term timetable, or face harsh penalties. Since 1972 only 41 firms have been debarred by the OFCCP for non-compliance, despite that many have not met goals.[42] Institutions must apply good-faith efforts to achieve diversity, but this does not mean that they must hire to fill quotas.[43]

The quota charge is based on a number of interacting factors. The economic vulnerability of the working and middle-class coincides with increased competition from previously marginalized groups and facilitates the perception of quotas. The presence of more minorities and women in employment institutions and whites' awareness of affirmative action, provide a further rationale for a belief in the existence of quotas. To economically troubled whites, it often appears that quotas must exist because their workplaces are now more diverse.

A NEW CONCEPTION OF EQUAL OPPORTUNITY

The defense of affirmative action presented in this study suggests that the public defense of affirmative action needs to facilitate a more genuine public understanding of equal opportunity. The entrenched, Lockean-inspired view of social equality posits that government and other societal institutions will ensure a level playing field by simply protecting contractual and legal rights. But Lockean notions overlook such factors as an individual's environmental and educational background, the criteria by which potential is discerned, and the reality that structural inequalities limit individual freedom for many *despite* laws which attempt to eliminate discrimination. By exposing the inadequacies of traditional selection criteria, and the persistence of racial, class, and gender discrimination, affirmative action defenders may foster an expanded view of equal opportunity. The old, yet lingering, American competitive marketplace model of equal opportunity establishes that the role of government is solely one of protecting individual rights, and then allowing individuals to achieve what they may in a fair, competitive marketplace. It is assumed that the individual's social, familial, and academic situation has little impact upon individual performance. Yet these factors *do affect* that pursuit of opportunity. Thus, assessing individual potential, especially that of racial minorities and the economically disadvantaged, through a limited and biased set of traditional criteria, particularly when other more relevant legitimate indicators could also be used, diminishes the life opportunities of the less fortunate.

A better conception of equal opportunity argues that government, academic, and employment institutions need to consider an individual's ability, or its potential, which may be obscured by traditional selection criteria. These establishments therefore must take positive steps to more fairly assess potential. This understanding of non-traditional modes of judging qualifications and potentiality strengthens the vulnerable, traditional defense of affirmative action, which is too often defended-solely-because of past discrimination and the need for intellectual and cultural diversity. The defenses, by themselves, fail to redefine the crucial concept of merit, and therefore, fail to publicly challenge the narrow and destructive liberal individualist predilection of American political culture.

NOTES

1. John David Skrentny, The *Ironies of Affirmative Action* (Chicago and London: The University of Chicago Press, 1996), chap.6.

2. See the *Philadelphia Inquirer*, March 16, 1995, Al. According to the federal government's Glass Ceiling Commission's 1995 report, ninety-five to ninety-seven percent of senior managers in the top thousand U.S. industrial companies and the five hundred biggest companies of all types are males. Prior to the federal government's efforts to promote female-owned business, which begun in the early 1980's these enterprises received a tiny proportion of federal-contract dollars, and in 1979 they were not awarded a single dollar! See the *Philadelphia Inquirer*, March 7, 1998.

3. A survey conducted by Jomills Henry Braddock II and James M. McPartland, see, "How Minorities Continue to be Excluded from Equal Employment Opportunities", *Journal of Social Issues*, Volume 43,1, (1987): Appendix, pp. 35–36, reveals that significant percentages of employers use tests, grades, and academic degrees for hiring and promoting. While a smaller number of employers rate traditional criteria as most important, and some do believe that recommendations and interviews are highly valuable for assessing applicants, it is unclear as to whether, or how often, companies evaluate candidates on a wide range of criteria.

4. It is clear that government enforcement of affirmative action is weak. See Barbara Bergmann, *In Defense of Affirmative Action* (New York: Basic Books, 1996), p. 44. It is , however, unclear to whether compliance assessments look at, or take seriously EEOC guidelines which require that selection methods be valid. See 29 CFR ch. XIV (7-1-96 Edition).

5. For a detailed discussion of affirmative action's successes see chapter 2,especially pp.7–9, 11–15.

6. For a discussion of the adverse impact of using only traditional criteria, see chapter two, pp. 5–11.

7. David Owen, None of the Above (Boston, Mass.: Houghton Mifflin Company, 1985), pp. 238–239.

8. Braddock and McPartland, "How Minorities Continue to be Excluded from Equal Employment Opportunities", pp. 35–36.

9. Alan Farnham, "Holding Firm on Affirmative Action", in Fortune, March 13, 1987, pp. 87–88.

10. 480 U.S. 149 (1987) at 160.

11. Ibid., at 156–163.

12. 401 U.S. 424 (1971) at 433.

13. 422 U.S. 405 (1975) at 431–433

14. 426 U.S. 229 (1976) at 250.

15. Ibid., at 251.

16. 401 U.S. 424 (1971) at 428.

17. 433 U.S. 321 (1977) at 331.

18. Ibid., at 336.

19. Ibid., at 336–337.

20. 440 U.S. 568 (1979) at 587–592.

21. Andrew Hacker, *Two Nations* (New York: Charles Scribner's Sons, 1992), p. 143. See also, Susan Strum and Lani Guinier, "The Future of Affirmative Action: Reclaiming the Innovative Ideal," *California Law Review*, Vol. 84, 4, (1996): 989.

22. Andrew Hacker, "Affirmative Action," *Dissent*, 212, Fall 1995:pp. 466–468.

23. Ibid.

24. Strum and Guinier, "The Future of Affirmative Action . . .", p.989.

25. Ibid.

26. *Philadelphia Inquirer*, March 16, 1995, Al.

27. Charles Moskos, "How Do They Do It?", *The New Republic*, August 5, 1991, p. 17.

28. Ibid.

29. *Philadelphia Inquirer*, November 25, 2004, A4.

30. *Philadelphia Inquirer*, July 20, 1995, All.

31. Barbara Ehrenreich, "Is The Middle Class Doomed?", in *New York Times Magazine*, September 7, 1986, pp. 50–51.

32. Douglas S. Massey and Nancy A. Denton*, American Apartheid*: *Segregation and the Making of the Underclass* (Cambridge, Mass.: Harvard University Press, 1993), pp. 154–155.

33. Richard D. Kahlenberg, *The Remedy* (New York: Basic Books, 1966), p.65.

34. See the Philadelphia Inquirer, June 29, 1998, A2. In 1966, six percent of young African-Americans held a four-year college degree, compared to thirteen percent currently.

35. Currently, only 63 percent of students graduate within 6 years of entering college. 46 percent of African-American students and 67 percent of whites graduate within 6 years. See *Philadelphia Inquirer*, June 16, 2004, A1.

36. As I discussed in chapter one, the post-*Griggs* Supreme Court cases, which develop the concept of business necessity hiring criteria, reveal that racial workforce disparities are not of themselves legal evidence of discrimination, nor do they automatically render the standards which produced them as invalid or unfair selection criteria.

37. *Washington Post*, March 9, 1991, A6.

38. *The Gallup Poll* (Wilmington Delaware: Scholarly Resources, Inc., 1996), p.216.

39. Cited in Orlando Patterson, *The Ordeal of Integration* (Washington, D.C.: Counterpoint, 1997), p.152.

40. Robert Emmet Long, Ed., *Affirmative Action*, in The Reference Shelf, Volume 68, Number 3, (New York: The H.W. Wilson Company, 1996), p. 35.

41. Barbara Bergmann*, In Defense of Affirmative Action* (New York: Basic Books, 1996), p.44.

42. Ibid., p.54.

43. J. Cooper, *Affirmative Action and Equal Employment Opportunity Guide* (Washington, D.C.: Cooper and Associates Inc., 1987), quoted in, John Edwards, *When Race Counts* (London: Routledge, 1995), p. 121.

Bibliography

Appiah, K.A., and A. Gutmann. *Color Conscious*. Princeton, N.J.: Princeton University Press, 1996.

Bates, Timothy. *Banking on Black Enterprise*. Washington, D.C.: Joint Center for Political and Economic Studies, 1993.

Barlett, D.L., and J.B. Steele. America: *What Went Wrong?* Kansas City: Andrews and Mcmeel, 1992.

Bawdon, D. L., and J.L. Palmer. "Challenging The Welfare State." In *The Reagan Record*, edited by John L. Palmer, Isabel V. Sawhill. Cambridge, Mass.: Ballinger Publishing Company, 1984.

Bell, Daniel. "On Meritocracy and Equality." *The Public Interest* 29 (1972): 29–68.

Bellah, R., R. Madsen, W.M. Sullivan, A. Swidler, and S. M. Tipton. *Habits of the Heart*. New York: Harper and Row, 1985.

Belz, Herman. *Equality Transformed*. New Brunswick, N.J.: Transaction Publishers, 1991.

Benokratis, N.V., and M.K. Gilbert. "Women in Federal Government Employment." In *Affirmative Action in Perspective*, edited by F.A. Blanchard, and F.J. Crosby. New York: Springer-Verlag, 1989.

Bergmann, Barbara. *In Defense of Affirmative Action*. New York: Basic Books, 1996.

Berry, Mary Frances. *Black Resistance, White Law*. New York: Meredith Corporation, 1971.

———. "How Percentage Plans Keep Minority Students Out of College." *Chronicle of Higher Education*, 4 August 2000, A 48.

Bloch, Farrell. *Antidiscrimination Law and Minority Employment*. Chicago: University of Chicago Press, 1994.

Bowen, W.G., and D. Bok. *The Shape of the River*. Princeton, N.J.: Princeton University Press, 1998.

Braddock, J.H. II, and J.M. McPartland. "How Minorities Continue to be Excluded from Equal Employment Opportunities." *Journal of Social Issues* 43:1 (1987): Appendix.

Brauer, C.M. *John F. Kennedy and the Second Reconstruction*. New York: Columbia University Press, 1977.

Bureau of National Affairs. *ABCs of The Equal Employment Opportunity Act*. Washington, D.C.: Bureau of National Affairs, 1972.

Burstein, Paul. *Discrimination, Jobs, and Politics*. Chicago: University of Chicago Press, 1985.

Cayer, N.J., and L. Sigelman. "Minorities and Women in State and Local Government: 1973–1975." *Public Administration Review* 40:5 (1980): 443–450.

Cohn, Samuel. *Race, Gender and Discrimination at Work*. Boulder, Colo.: Westview Press, 2000.

Congressional Quarterly. *1980 Congressional Quarterly Almanac*. Washington, D.C.: Congressional Quarterly, 1981.

———. *Congress and the Nation*. Volume 3. Washington, D.C.: Congressional Quarterly, 1973.

Crosby, F., and C. Van De Veer, eds. *Sex, Race and Merit*. Ann Arbor: The University of Michigan Press, 2000.

Cross, Theodore. "What If There Was No Affirmative Action in College Admissions? A Further Refinement of Our Earlier Conclusions." In *The Journal of Blacks in Higher Education* 5 (Autumn 1994): 52–55.

Crouse, J., and D. Trusheim. *The Case Against the SAT*. Chicago: University of Chicago Press, 1988.

Detlefsen, Robert R. *Civil Rights Under Reagan*. San Francisco: ICS Press, 1991.

Dworkin, Ronald. "Are Quotas Unfair?" In *Racial Preference and Racial Justice*, edited by Russell Nieli. Washington, D.C.: Ethics and Public Policy Center, 1991.

Dreier, R., and R. Freer. "Saints, Sinners, and Affirmative Action." *The Chronicle of Higher Education*, 24 October 1997, B6-B7.

Eastland, Terry. *Ending Affirmative Action*. New York: Basic Books, 1996.

Edwards, Jonathan. *When Race Counts*. London and New York: Routledge, 1995.

Ezorsky, Gertrude. *Racism and Justice*. Ithaca, N.Y.: Cornell University Press, 1991.

Farnham, Alan. "Holding Firm on Affirmative Action." *Fortune*, 13 March 1989, 89–88.

Fletcher, Arthur. *The Silent Sell-Out*. New York: The Third Press, 1974.

Gamson, W.A., and A. Modigiliani. "The Changing Culture of Affirmative Action." *Research in Political Sociology* 3 (1987): 170.

Glazer, Nathan. "A Breakdown in Civil Rights Enforcement?" *The Public Interest* Spring (1971).

———. "Are Academic Standards Obsolete?" *Change* 2 (1972): 160.

———. *Affirmative Discrimination*. New York: Basic Books, 1975.

———. *Ethnic Dilemmas 1964–1972*. Cambridge, Mass.: Harvard University Press, 1983.

Graham, Hugh Davis. *The Civil Rights Era*. New York: Oxford University Press, 1990.

Granovetter, Mark. *Getting a Job*. Cambridge, Mass.: Harvard University Press, 1974.

Gutmann, A., and D. Thompson. *Democracy and Disagreement*. Cambridge, Mass.: Harvard University Press, 1996.

Hacker, Andrew. *Two Nations*. New York: Charles Scribner's Sons, 1992.

————. "Affirmative Action." *Dissent* 212 (1996): 466–468.

Hartigan, J.A., and A.K. Wigdor, eds. *Fairness In Employment Testing*. Washington, D.C.: National Academy Press, 1989.

Hartz, Lewis. From *The Liberal Tradition in America*. In *The American Polity Reader*, edited by A.G. Serow, W.W. Shannon, and E.C. Ladd. New York: W.W. Norton and Company, 1993.

Harvey, James C. *Black Civil Rights During the Johnson Administration*. Jackson, Miss.: University and College Press of Mississippi, 1973.

Hodgkinson, Harold. "What Shall We Call People." *Phi Beta Kappan* (October 1995): 176.

Holzer, H., and D. Neumark. "Are Affirmative Action Hires Less Qualified? Evidence from Employer-Employee Data on New Hires." *Journal of Labor Economics* 17:3 (1999): 557.

Hook, Sydney. "Discrimination, Color Blindness, and the Quota System." In *Reverse Discrimination*, edited by Barry R. Gross. Buffalo, N.Y.: Prometheus Books, 1977.

Horn, C.L., and S.M. Flores. *Percent Plans in College Admissions: A Comparative Analysis of Three States' Expereinces*. Cambridge: The Civil Rights Project, 2002.

Ingraham, P.W., and D.H. Rosenbloom, eds. *The Promise and Paradox of Civil Service Reform*. Pittsburgh, PA.: University of Pittsburgh Press, 1992.

Jaynes, G. and R. Williams, eds. *A Common Destiny: Blacks and American Society*. Washington, D.C.: National Academy Press, 1989.

Johnson, Lyndon B. *Public Papers of the Presidents*. Vol. 2. Washington, D.C.: Government Printing Office, 1965.

Khalenberg, Richard D. "Class, Not Race." *The New Republic*, 3 April 1995, 21–27.

————. *The Remedy*. New York: Basic Books, 1996.

Karabel, Jerome. "Stuck in the Station." *The Nation*, 15 December 1997, 222.

Kellough, J. Edward. *Federal Equal Employment Opportunity Policy and Numerical Goals and Timetables*. New York: Praeger, 1989.

————. "Affirmative Action in Government Employment." In *THE ANNALS of the American Academy of Political and Social Science*. Volume 523, edited by H. Orlans, and J. O'Neil. Newbury Park: SAGE Publications, Inc., 1992.

Kellough, J.E., and D.H. Rosenbloom. "Representative Bureaucracy and the EEOC: Did Civil Service Reform Make a Difference?" In *The Promise and Paradox of Civil Service Reform*, edited by P.W. Ingraham, and D.H. Rosenbloom. Pittsburgh, PA.: University of Pittsburgh Press, 1992.

Kirschenmann, J., and K.M. Neckerman. "We'd Love to Hire Them, But . . .: The Meaning of Race for Employers." In *The Urban Underclass*, edited by C. Jencks, and P.E. Peterson. Washington, D.C.: Brookings Institution, 1996.

Klitgaard, Robert. *Choosing Elites*. New York: Basic Books, 1985.

Krislov, Samuel. 1967. *The Negro in Federal Employment*. Minneapolis, Minn.: Univesrity of Minnesota Press, 1967.

LaNoue, George R. "Split Visions: Minority Business Set-Asides." In *THE ANNALS of the American Academy of Political and Social Science*. Volume 523, edited by H. Orlans, and J. O'Neil. Newbury Park: SAGE Publications, Inc., 1992.

Leonard, Jonathan. "The Impact of Affirmative Action on Employment." In *Racial Preference and Racial Justice*, edited by Russell Nieli. Washington, D.C.: Ethics and Public Policy Center, 1991.

Lewis, Michael. *The Culture of Inequality*. Amherst: Univesrity of Massachusetts Press, 1978.

Lipset, Seymour Martin. "Equal Chances versus Equal Rights." In *THE ANNALS of the American Academy of Political and Social Science*. Volume 523, edited by H. Orlans, and J. O'Neil. Newbury Park: SAGE Publications, Inc., 1992.

Locke, John. *The Second Treatise of Government*. New York: Macmillian, 1952.

Long, Robert Emmett., ed. *Affirmative Action*. Volume 68, N. 3, *The Reference Shelf*. New York: H.W. Wilson, 1996.

Loury, Glenn. "Beyond Civil Rights." In *Racial Preference and Racial Justice*, edited by Russell Nieli. Washington, D.C.: Ethics and Public Policy Center, 1991.

Lovrich, N.P., Jr., and B.S. Steel. "Affirmative Action and Productivity in Law Enforcement Agencies." *Review of Public Personnel Administration* 4 (1980): 55–65.

Lovrich, N.P., Jr., B.S. Steel, and K.Hood. "Equity Versus Productivity: Affirmative Action and Municipal Police Services." *Public Productivity Review* 39 (1986): 61–70.

Lynch, Frederick R. "Affirmative Action, the Media, and the Public." *American Behavioral Scientist* 28 (1985): 807–827.

Marin, P. and E.K. Lee. *Appearance and Reality in the Sunshine State: The Talented 20 Program in Florida*. Cambridge: The Civil Rights Project, 2002.

Massey, D.S., and N.A. Denton. *American Apartheid*. Cambridge, Mass.: Harvard University Press, 1993.

McCloskey, H., and J. Zaller. *The American Ethos.* . Cambridge, Mass.: Harvard University Press, 1984.

McMullen, Liz. "Policies Said to Help Companies Hire Qualified Workers at No Extra Cost." *The Chronicle of Higher Education*, 17 November 1995, A7.

Miller, W., and S.A. Traugott. *American National Election Studies Data Source Book*. Cambridge, Mass.: Harvard University Press, 1989.

Mladenka, Kenneth R. "Blacks and Hispanics in Urban Politics." *American Political Science Review* 83: 1 (1989): 165–189.

Mosley, A.G., and N. Capaldi. *Affirmative Action*. New York: Rowman and Littlefield, 1996.

Moskos, C.C., and J.S. Butler. *All That We Can Be*. New York: Basic Books, 1996.

Moskos, Charles C. "How Do They Do It?" *The New Republic*. 16 March 1991, 16–20.

NaCoste, Rupert W. "Affirmative Action and Self-Evaluation." In *Affirmative Action in Perspective*, edited by F.A. Blanchard and F.J. Crosby. New York: Springer-Verlag, 1989.

Nathan, Richard P. *Jobs and Civil Rights*. Washington, D.C.: U.S. Government Printing Office, 1969.

Nichols, Michael P. 1984. *Family Therapy*. New York: Gardner Press, 1984.

Orlans, H. "Affirmative Action in Higher Education." In *THE ANNALS of the American Academy of Political and Social Science*. Volume 523, edited by H. Orlans, and J. O'Neil. Newbury Park: SAGE Publications, Inc., 1992.

Orr, Eleanor W. *Twice as Less*. New York: Norton, 1987.

Owen, David. *None of the Above*. Boston, Mass.: Hougton Mifflin, 1985.

Patterson, Orlando. *The Ordeal of Integration*. Washington, D.C.: Counterpoint, 1997.

Pavela, Gary. "What's Wrong with Race-based Affirmative Action?" In *Responding to the New Affirmative Action Climate*, edited by Donald D. Gehring. San Francisco: Jossey-Bass Publishers, 1998.

Peterson, G.E. and W.P. Vroman. "Urban Labor Markets and Economic Opportunity." In *Urban Markets and Job Opportunity*, edited by G.E. Peterson and W.P. Vroman. Washington, D.C.: Urban Institute Press, 1992.

Plano J.C., and M. Greenberg. *The American Political Dictionary*. Ninth ed. Fort Worth, Texas: Harcourt Brace College Publisher, 1990.

Pottinger, J.Stanley. "The Drive Toward Equality." In *Reverse Discrimination*, edited by B.R. Gross. Buffalo, N.Y.: Prometheus Books, 1977.

Preer, Jean L. *Lawyers V. Educators*. Westport, Conn.: Greenwood Press, 1982.

Robertson, D.B., and D.R. Judd. *The Development of American Public Policy*. Glenview, Illinois: Scott, Foresman and Company, 1989.

Rodgers, Harrell, R., Jr. "Fair Employment Laws for Minorities." In *Implementation of Civil Rights Policy*, edited by C.S. Bullock, III, and C.M. Lamb. Monterey, Cal.: Brooks/Cole Publishing, 1984.

Rosenbloom, David H. *Federal Equal Employment Opportunity*. New York: Praeger, 1977.

Safire, William. *Before the Fall*. New York: Da Capo Press, 1975.

Schuman, H., C. Steeh, L. Bobo, and M. Krysan. *Racial Attitudes in America: Trends and Interpretations*. Cambridge, Mass.: Harvard University Press, 1997.

Schwartz, Bernard. *Behind Bakke*. New York: New York University Press, 1988.

Sharf, James C. "Litigating Personnel Measurement Policy." *Journal of Vocational Behavior* (December 1988): 239–254.

Sher, George. "Qualification, Fairness, and Desert." In *Equal Opportunity*, edited by Norman E. Bowie. Boulder, Colo.: Westview Press, 1988.

Shuford, Bettina. "Recommendations for the Future." In *Responding to the New Affirmative Action Climate*, edited by Donald D. Gehring. San Francisco: Jossey-Bass Publishers, 1998.

Shull, Steven A. *A Kinder, Gentler Racism?* Armonk, New York: M.E. Sharpe, 1993.

Sigelman, L., and S. Welch. *Black Americans' Views of Racial Inequality*. Cambridge: Cambridge University Press, 1991.

Skrentny, John David. *The Ironies of Affirmative Action*. Chicago, Ill.: University of Chicago Press, 1996.

Sniderman, P. and T. Piazza. *The Scar of Race*. Cambridge, Mass.: Harvard University Press, 1993.

Sowell, Thomas. "Are Quotas Good for Blacks?" In *Racial Preference and Racial Justice*, edited by Russell Nieli. Washington, D.C.: Ethics and Public Policy Center, 1991.

Stein, Lana. "Representative Local Government: Minorities in the Municipal Work Force." *The Journal of Politics* 48 (1986): 694–711.

Sturm, S., and L. Guinier. "The Future of Affirmative Action: Reclaiming the Innovative Ideal." *California Law Review* 84: 4 (1996): 987–992.

Thernstrom, S., and A. Thernstrom. *America in Black and White*. New York. Simon and Schuster, 1997.

Torres, G., and P.D. Hair. "The Texas Test Case: Integrating America's Colleges." *The Chronicle of Higher Education*, 4 October 2000, B6.

Tuch, S.A., and J.K. Martin, eds. *Racial Attitudes in the 1990's: Continuity and Change*. Cambridge, Mass.: Harvard University Press, 1997.

Turner, M.A., M. Fix, and R.J. Struyk. *Opportunities Denied, Opportunities Diminished*. Washington, D.C.: The Urban Institute Press, 1991.

U.S. Civil Service Commission. *Study of Minority Group Employment in the Federal Government: 1965*. Washington, D.C.: Government Printing Office, 1965.

U.S. Commission on Civil Rights. *For All the People . . . By All the People*. Washington, D.C.: Government Printing Office, 1969.

U.S. Congress, Senate Subcommittee on Separation of Powers of the Senate Committee on the Judiciary. 1969. *Hearings on The Philadelphia Plan and S. 931. 91st Congress, 1st session.*

U.S. Department of Labor. *OFCCP Quick Facts*. Washington, D.C.: U.S. Department of Labor.

Walzer, Michael. "In Defense of Equality." *Dissent* 20 (1973): 399–408.

———. *Spheres of Justice*. New York: Basic Books, 1983.

Wigdor, A.K., and W.R. Garner, eds. *Ability Testing: Uses, Consequences, and Controversies, Part 1*. Washington, D.C.: National Academy Press, 1982.

Wigdor, A.K., and B.F. Green, Jr., eds. *Performance Assessment for the Workplace*. Vol. 1. Washington, D.C.: National Academy Press, 1991.

Wightman, Linda F. "The Threat to Diversity in Legal Education: An Empirical Analysis of the Consequences of Abandoning Race as a Factor in Law School Admissions Decisions." *New York University Law Review* 72:1 (1997): 4–5, 36.

Wilson, William J. *The Truly Disadvantaged*. Chicago: University of Chicago Press, 1987.

———. *When Work Disappears*. New York: Alfred A. Knopf, 1997.

Young, Iris M. *Justice and the Politics of Difference*. Princeton, N.J.: Princeton, University Press, 1990.

Index

abstract individualism, 8, 10, 20–21, 36
Adarand v. Mineta. See affirmative
    action; public contracts
Adarand v. Pena. See affirmative action;
    public contracts
affirmative action: alternatives to,
    61–62; class-based, 49–58; diversity
    defense, 12–14, 18, 41–42, 81;
    gender, 58–61; in higher education,
    12–14, 18, 28–32, 41–43, 50–52,
    85–86; as hot button issue, 4–7,
    17–18, 62–64, 90–95; impacts of
    rollbacks in higher education, 29–33;
    in Johnson administration, 3–5; in
    Kennedy administration, 1–3, 7–8;
    for middle class blacks, 50–54; in
    Nixon administration, 5–7, 8–10;
    origins of controversy, 4–11; past
    discrimination defense, 8–10, 42;
    positive results of, 33–35; as
    preferential treatment, 6–12, 28,
    60–61, 94; in public contracts, 5–6,
    8–9, 17, 34–35, 57–58; as creating
    quotas, 6,12,15,94–95; reverse
    discrimination critique,
    6,12,79,93–94; rollbacks to, 14–15,
    17–18; as second best policy, xi, 64;
    self respect critique, 42–44, 92–93;
    vulnerability of, 17–18

Albemarle v. Moody, 83–84
American political culture, vi–viii, x, 8,
    10, 13, 19–21, 36; ideological limits
    of, 66–68, 70, 91, 95. *See also*
    abstract individualism

Bates, Timothy, 35
Bell, Daniel, vii–viii, x
Bellah, Robert. *See* American Political
    Culture
Bergmann, Barbara, 73n50, 96n4, 97n41
Berry, Mary F., 1
Bowen, William G., 29–32, 55
Braddock, Jomills H., 27, 40, 52, 82
Brauer, Carl M., 2, 8
Bush, George H.W., 62
Bush, George W., 77, 86
business necessity standard. *See*
    Griggs v. Duke Power; Civil
    Rights Act of 1991; *Wards Cove v.
    Antonio*

California Civil Rights Initiative
    (CCRI). *See* Proposition 209
Carter, Jimmy, 60
City of Richmond v. J.A. Crosson, 17
Civil Rights Act of 1964, 4;
    amendments to Title VII, 4–5, 7–8;
    merit concerns, 4–5, 7–8

105